토익 스피킹 **실전 모의고사 15회**

지은이 한수종(Stella)
펴낸이 임상진
펴낸곳 (주)넥서스

초판 1쇄 발행 2013년 8월 20일
초판 11쇄 발행 2018년 5월 15일

출판신고 1992년 4월 3일 제311-2002-2호
10880 경기도 파주시 지목로 5
Tel (02)330-5500 Fax (02)330-5555

ISBN 978-89-6790-453-1 13740

저자와 출판사의 허락 없이 내용의 일부를
인용하거나 발췌하는 것을 금합니다.

가격은 뒤표지에 있습니다.
잘못 만들어진 책은 구입처에서 바꾸어 드립니다.

www.nexusbook.com

최신 기출을 완벽하게 반영한

토익 스피킹 실전 모의고사 15회

Stella 지음

넥서스

머리말

변함없이 토익 스피킹 강의 현장 속으로 발걸음을 내딛는다. 오늘도 레벨 6에 7 또는 만점을 받겠다는 다짐을 가진 학생들로 강의실이 북적거린다. 그들을 볼 때마다 나 또한 엄숙한 조덕자가 되어 목표 달성을 돕고 싶다는 강한 의욕을 느낀다. 그것이 내가 스파르타 방식의 점수 보장 체제 수업을 고집하는 이유가 아닐까 한다. 직접 가르친 수강생들이 80% 이상이 목표를 달성하는 것을 보면서 토익 스피킹 공부에 정도(正道)가 있다는 것을 다시 한 번 깨닫게 된다. 그래서 〈토익 스피킹 실전 모의고사 15회〉를 통해 본인의 방법을 함께 공유하고자 한다.

1. 단순 암기 방식은 통하지 않는다.

토익 스피킹은 회화 능력을 측정하는 시험이다. 하루도 거르지 않고 꾸준히 공부하는 학습 진리가 여기에서도 통한다. 단순 암기가 아닌 자신의 영어 실력이 있어야 목표 달성에 성큼 다가갈 수 있다. 물론 토스의 유형과 답변 방식도 잘 알고 있어야 한다.

2. 무한 반복한다.

2주 안에 단순 암기가 아닌 영어 실력을 늘리려면 다음의 3가지를 무한 반복하고 기억하자.

첫째, 크게 소리 내어 계속 읽는다.

자신의 레벨보다 약간 높은 수준의 답변을 읽는다. 이때, 절대로 답변을 외워서는 안 되고, 본인이 실제로 답변하고 있는 듯한 느낌으로 읽어야 한다.

둘째, 활용 가능한 어휘를 자주 접한다.

새로운 어휘를 공부하기보다는 이미 알고 있는데 입에서 맴돌던 수준의 어휘를 쓸 수 있도록 나는 다양한 표현들을 내 것으로 만들어야 한다. 다른 경험으로 알겠지만 내에게 생소한 어휘는 긴장이 극대화되는 시험 상황에서는 절대 입 밖으로 나오지 않는다. 현재 나의 수준에서 충분히 쓸 수 있지만 놓치고 있는 어휘들만 공부한다.

셋째, 쓰지 말고 말하라.

글로 쓰지 않고 입으로 직접 답을 만드는 연습을 충분히 하면 우리의 뇌가 이 과정을 하나의 회로로 인지하게 된다. 지금껏 영어 공부를 할 때 무조건 필기를 끊임없이 쓴 건 사실이다. 그런데 여러분이 회화 실력은 어떠한가? 자전거 타는 법이 우리 몸에 자연스럽게 배어 익숙해지는 것처럼 영어 말하기가 또한 자연스럽게 입으로 하는 연습을 해 보자.

위 방법을 명심하고, 본 교재에서 실제 목표 레벨이 답변 수준을 확인하도록 하자. 또, 유형을 완전 숙지하고 모의고사 14회를 위와 같은 방식으로 2주간 공부한 후, 최종 점검으로 남은 모의고사 1회를 푸는 방식으로 활용하면 된다.

마지막으로 이 책이 나오기까지 애쓰신 에씨스 영어교재팀, 집필 과정을 함께한 인텐시브 스터디 멤버들, 특히 준이, 예슬이, 현석이, 무엇보다 지금까지 열심히 내조해 준 우리 남편 이동민 씨, 그리고 사랑하는 가족에게 무한한 감사의 마음을 전한다.

Stella

목차

Contents

머리말	4
구성과 특징	6
토익 스피킹이란?	7
레벨별 목표 차방전 & 토익 스피킹에 관한 오해와 진실	8

Actual Test 01	10
Actual Test 02	17
Actual Test 03	24
Actual Test 04	31
Actual Test 05	38
Actual Test 06	45
Actual Test 07	52
Actual Test 08	59
Actual Test 09	66
Actual Test 10	73
Actual Test 11	80
Actual Test 12	87
Actual Test 13	94
Actual Test 14	101
Actual Test 15	108

책속책 | 정답 및 해설 + 스텔라 쌤의 파트별 필수 공략법

구성과 특징

Structure & Features

1. 최신 기출 경향을 완벽하게 반영한 기출모의 15회

마치 실제 시험 보는 것처럼 실전의 경향과 유형을 가장 잘 반영한 최종 점검 문제

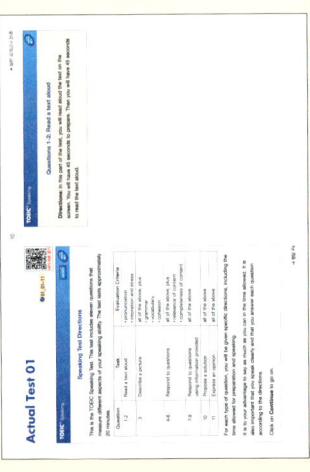

2. 스티믈라 쌤의 파트별 필수 공략법

토익 스피킹 전문가의 파트별 핵심 노하우와 고득점 비법 전수

3. 실제 시험 환경을 재현한 온라인 테스트 _ www.nexusbook.com

교재의 문제를 실제 토익 스피킹 시험 화면과 가장 유사한 환경으로 풀어 보는 온라인 모의 테스트

4. 샘플 문제와 레벨별 학습자들의 생생한 육성 답변

문제 / 답변 / MP3 무료 다운로드 (www.nexusbook.com & QR코드)

샘플 문제와 Level 6, 7, 8 학습자들의 생생한 육성 답변을 통해 유형을 익히고 나의 수준 파악

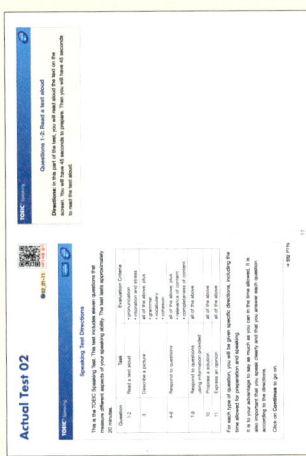

5. 학습자의 눈높이에 맞춘 정답

모든 문제에 대한 정답뿐. 브레인스토밍 제시 및 눈높이에 맞는 현실적인 답변 수록

6. 모의고사 15회 문제와 답변 MP3 무료 다운로드

www.nexusbook.com & QR코드

원어민의 목소리로 녹음한 모든 문제와 답변 MP3 음원을 홈페이지에서 무료 다운로드하거나 QR코드로 간편하게 듣기

토익 스피킹이란?

TOEIC Speaking은 TOEIC 시험을 개발한 비영리 시험 개발 기관인 ETS(Educational Testing Service)에서 개발한 말하기 능력 측정 시험이다. 업무와 관련된 상황 혹은 일상생활에서 수험자에야 할 과제에 관련된 문제가 출제된다.

✪ 시험 구성

총 6개 파트, 11개 문제로 구성되어 있으며, 시험은 약 20분 정도 소요된다. 문제별 시험 구성은 다음과 같다.

구분	문제 유형	문항 수	시간
Part 1 Questions 1-2	Read a text aloud 문장 읽기	2	답변 시간 45초 준비 시간 45초
Part 2 Question 3	Describe a picture 사진 묘사	1	답변 시간 45초 준비 시간 30초
Part 3 Questions 4-6	Respond to questions 듣고 질문에 답하기	3	답변 시간 15 ~ 30초 준비 시간 없음
Part 4 Questions 7-9	Respond to questions using information provided 제공된 정보를 사용하여 질문에 답하기	3	답변 시간 15 ~ 30초 준비 시간 없음 (자료 읽는 시간 30초)
Part 5 Question 10	Propose a solution 해결책 제안하기	1	답변 시간 60초 준비 시간 30초
Part 6 Question 11	Express an opinion 의견 제시하기	1	답변 시간 60초 준비 시간 15초

✪ 시험 평가 기준

1~9번 문제는 0~3점, 10~11번 문제는 0~5점 범위 내에서 평가되며, 채점 결과는 0~200점 범위로 환산되어 10점 단위로 표시된다. 문제별 평가 기준은 다음과 같다.

구분	평가 기준	
Questions 1-2	• 발음	• 억양과 강세
Question 3	위의 모든 항목에 더하여	• 문법 • 어휘 • 일관성
Questions 4-6	위의 모든 항목에 더하여	• 내용의 일관성 • 내용의 완성도
Questions 7-11	위의 모든 항목	

✪ 시험 접수와 응시료

시험은 인터넷 홈페이지(www.toeicspeaking.co.kr)를 통해서만 접수할 수 있다. 응시료는 부가세 10%를 포함하여 77,000원이며, Writing Test를 함께 응시할 경우 부가세 10% 포함 104,500원의 할인된 가격으로 응시할 수 있다. 인터넷 접수 시 비용 결제는 신용 카드 또는 실시간 계좌 이체를 통해 가능하다.

✪ 성적 확인

시험 응시일로부터 약 10일 후 인터넷 홈페이지(www.toeic.co.kr)를 통해 확인할 수 있다. 성적표는 온라인과 우편을 통해 수령 가능하며, 온라인 성적 발급의 경우 인터넷 홈페이지를 통해 성적과 함께 즉시 발급할 수 있다. 우편 수령 신청자의 경우 성적 발표일으로부터 7~10일 이내에 성적표를 받아볼 수 있다.

✪ 수험자 유의 사항

반드시 입실 시간을 엄수해야 하며, 입실 통제 시간 이후에는 입실이 불가하다. 시험 당일 인정되는 신분증은 주민등록증, 운전면허증, 여권, 공무원증이며 규정 신분증을 지참하지 않은 수험자는 시험에 응시할 수 없다.

✪ 시험 일정

정기시험은 매주 1회, 연간 48회 시행되며, 1일 총 3~4회의 시험이 진행된다. 그러나 상황에 따라 추가 시험이 시행되기도 한다.

토익 스피킹에 관한 오해와 진실

1. 수준 높은 어휘만 써야 고득점을 얻을 수 있다?

무조건 어려운 어휘만을 말해야 높은 점수를 받는 것은 아니다. 레벨 8 이상의 점수를 목표로 한다면 CNN 같은 해외 뉴스에서 쓰는 어휘를 몇 개 사용하는 것도 좋다. 하지만 레벨 7 이하의 점수를 목표로 한다면 쉬운 표현이라도 상황에 맞게 논리적으로 쓰는 것이 더 중요하다.

2. 높은 레벨을 받으려면 최소 영미권 어학연수는 필수다?

토익 스피킹은 회화라기보다는 문제 유형이 정해진 듯기가 시험이다. 영미권 유학을 얼마나 분석하고 준비했는지가 고득점의 관건이다. 그러므로 이해하고 있는지, 문제 유형을 얼마나 분석하고 준비했는지가 고득점의 관건이다. 그러므로 영미 문화권에서의 체류 여부가 점수를 결정짓지는 않는다.

3. 발음이 원어민처럼 좋으면 높은 레벨을 딸 수 있다?

레벨을 잘 받기 위해서는 원어민 같은 발음과 유창함을 겸비하면 좋다. 그러나 영어가 모어가 아닌 이상 상대방과 의사소통이 가능할 정도의 명확한 발음과 유창함만 있으면 된다. 물론 의미를 전달하는 데 문제가 있을 만큼 발음이 좋지 않다면 자신의 목소리를 녹음해서 까다롭거나 잘 고쳐지지 않는 발음은 반복적으로 연습하자.

레벨별 목표 달성 처방전

1. Level 6 목표자

대상	Level 5 점수대의 학습자
증상	영어 스피킹에 어려움이 있으나 간단한 단어나 암기한 문장으로 대강 표현할 수 있다.
처방전	1. 단문의 모범 답안을 반복하여 외운다. (Q. 3 Describe a picture과 Q. 4~6 Respond to Questions) 2. 영작부터 하지 말고 영어로 바로 말하는 연습을 한다. 3. 무조건 다 표현하겠다는 욕심보다는 실력이 범위 내에서 답변하려고 노력한다.

2. Level 7 목표자

대상	Level 6 점수대의 학습자
증상	풀어 본 문제 유형이 출제되었거나 준비 시간만 충분하면 의견을 잘 전달할 수 있는 수준이다.
처방전	1. 각 파트의 대표 유형의 모범 답안을 반복하여 읽으며 빈출 표현과 문장을 익힌다. 2. 새롭거나 어려운 어휘에 집중하지 말고 이미 알고 있는 어휘들을 숙달하게 익힌다. (Q. 10 Propose a solution과 Q. 11 Express an opinion) 3. 모두에게 주어진 시간은 똑같다. 시간 관리에 좀 더 신경 쓴다.

3. Level 8 목표자

대상	Level 7 점수대의 학습자
증상	전달하려는 내용을 잘 표현하는 편이나 다양하지 않고 제한적이다.
처방전	1. 각 파트별 대표 문제들과 그 유형에서 파생될 수 있는 주제, 표현들까지 모두 꼼꼼하게 정리하고 말하는 연습을 한다. 2. 난이도가 높고 새로운 어휘를 접할 수 있는 다양한 교재를 반복하여 읽는다.

Actual Test

- Actual Test 01
- Actual Test 02
- Actual Test 03
- Actual Test 04
- Actual Test 05
- Actual Test 06
- Actual Test 07
- Actual Test 08
- Actual Test 09
- Actual Test 10
- Actual Test 11
- Actual Test 12
- Actual Test 13
- Actual Test 14
- Actual Test 15

MP3 바로듣기

Actual Test 01

TOEIC® Speaking

Speaking Test Directions

This is the TOEIC Speaking Test. This test includes eleven questions that measure different aspects of your speaking ability. The test lasts approximately 20 minutes.

Question	Task	Evaluation Criteria
1-2	Read a text aloud	• pronunciation • intonation and stress
3	Describe a picture	all of the above, plus • grammar • vocabulary • cohesion
4-6	Respond to questions	all of the above, plus • relevance of content • completeness of content
7-9	Respond to questions using information provided	all of the above
10	Propose a solution	all of the above
11	Express an opinion	all of the above

For each type of question, you will be given specific directions, including the time allowed for preparation and speaking.

It is to your advantage to say as much as you can in the time allowed. It is also important that you speak clearly and that you answer each question according to the directions.

Click on **Continue** to go on.

TOEIC® Speaking

Questions 1-2: Read a text aloud

Directions: In this part of the test, you will read aloud the text on the screen. You will have 45 seconds to prepare. Then you will have 45 seconds to read the text aloud.

Question 1 of 11

This is Jack. Here's the weather forecast. We have beautiful weather here for this weekend. We will have sunny skies and highs will be above 26°C overnight. But temperatures are dropping down into the -2°C. And we have got big changes ahead for the upcoming work week starting tomorrow. By Thursday, temperatures may not get out of the thirties. These hot summer temperatures will remain for a couple more days.

PREPARATION TIME
00:00:45

RESPONSE TIME
00:00:45

Question 2 of 11

Welcome to Commonwealth Bank's orientation for new employees. I am Max Chow, and I am the CFO of the bank. It is an honor for me to introduce the bank's vision for 2013 to you. We have been leading the financial field for the past 10 years in a row. I am sure you will grow along with the bank. In just a moment, your trainers will distribute the schedule for this week's training.

PREPARATION TIME
00:00:45

RESPONSE TIME
00:00:45

Question 3: Describe a picture

Directions: In this part of the test, you will describe the picture on your screen in as much detail as you can. You will have 30 seconds to prepare your response. Then you will have 45 seconds to speak about the picture.

Question 3 of 11

PREPARATION TIME
00:00:30

RESPONSE TIME
00:00:45

TOEIC® Speaking

Questions 4-6: Respond to questions

Directions: In this part of the test, you will answer three questions. For each question, begin responding immediately after you hear a beep. No preparation time is provided. You will have 15 seconds to respond to Questions 4 and 5 and 30 seconds to respond to Question 6.

TOEIC® Speaking

Question 4 of 11

Imagine that an Australian marketing firm is doing research in your country. You have agreed to participate in a telephone interview about a travel bag.

Where do you usually buy a travel bag?

RESPONSE TIME
00:00:15

TOEIC® Speaking

Question 5 of 11

Imagine that an Australian marketing firm is doing research in your country. You have agreed to participate in a telephone interview about a travel bag.

Do you want to buy a new one or a used one?

RESPONSE TIME
00:00:15

TOEIC® Speaking

Question 6 of 11

Imagine that an Australian marketing firm is doing research in your country. You have agreed to participate in a telephone interview about a travel bag.

What do you consider first when you buy a travel bag?

- Color
- Size
- Price

RESPONSE TIME
00:00:30

TOEIC® Speaking

Questions 7-9: Respond to questions using information provided

Directions: In this part of the test, you will answer three questions based on the information provided. You will have 30 seconds to read the information before the questions begin. For each question, begin responding immediately after you hear a beep. No additional preparation time is provided. You will have 15 seconds to respond to Questions 7 and 8 and 30 seconds to respond to Question 9.

TOEIC® Speaking

Business Trip Itinerary

Chris Lee, HSC Company Sales Department

Departure From	Departure Date	Destination	Arrival Date	Flight/Train	Accommodations
London	10/23	New York	10/24	UK Air AF 343	Broadway Hotel
New York	10/26	Chicago	10/26	Express Train	Chicago Art Hotel
Chicago	10/29	Hong Kong	10/30	Pacific Air QE 304	Hillside Hotel
Hong Kong	11/4	London	11/5	UK Air AB 349	

* All hotels provide free shuttle buses from the airport to the hotel.
* Please call to confirm your final schedule at least one week prior to departure. Any change in itinerary requires notification by phone. (ext. 986)

PREPARATION TIME
00:00:30

Business Trip Itinerary

Chris Lee, HSC Company Sales Department

Departure From	Departure Date	Destination	Arrival Date	Flight/Train	Accommodations
London	10/23	New York	10/24	UK Air AF 343	Broadway Hotel
New York	10/26	Chicago	10/26	Express Train	Chicago Art Hotel
Chicago	10/29	Hong Kong	10/30	Pacific Air QE 304	Hillside Hotel
Hong Kong	11/4	London	11/5	UK Air AB 349	

* All hotels provide free shuttle buses from the airport to the hotel.
* Please call to confirm your final schedule at least one week prior to departure. Any change in itinerary requires notification by phone. (ext. 986)

RESPONSE TIME 00:00:15

Question 10: Propose a solution

Directions: In this part of the test, you will be presented with a problem and asked to propose a solution. You will have 30 seconds to prepare. Then you will have 60 seconds to speak.

In your response, be sure to
- show that you recognize the problem, and
- propose a way of dealing with the problem.

Business Trip Itinerary

Chris Lee, HSC Company Sales Department

Departure From	Departure Date	Destination	Arrival Date	Flight/Train	Accommodations
London	10/23	New York	10/24	UK Air AF 343	Broadway Hotel
New York	10/26	Chicago	10/26	Express Train	Chicago Art Hotel
Chicago	10/29	Hong Kong	10/30	Pacific Air QE 304	Hillside Hotel
Hong Kong	11/4	London	11/5	UK Air AB 349	

* All hotels provide free shuttle buses from the airport to the hotel.
* Please call to confirm your final schedule at least one week prior to departure. Any change in itinerary requires notification by phone. (ext. 986)

RESPONSE TIME
00:00:30

TOEIC® Speaking

Question 11: Express an opinion

Directions: In this part of the test, you will give your opinion about a specific topic. Be sure to say as much as you can in the time allowed. You will have 15 seconds to prepare. Then you will have 60 seconds to speak.

TOEIC® Speaking

Question 11 of 11

Some companies prefer to hire experienced workers to increase productivity rather than young and inexperienced workers. Which do you prefer and why? Use specific reasons or examples to support your opinion.

PREPARATION TIME
00:00:15

RESPONSE TIME
00:01:00

TOEIC® Speaking

Question 10 of 11

TOEIC® Speaking

Question 10 of 11

Respond as if you are the sales director of the company.

In your response, be sure to
- show that you recognize the problem, and
- propose a way of dealing with the problem.

PREPARATION TIME
00:00:30

RESPONSE TIME
00:01:00

Actual Test 02

Speaking Test Directions

This is the TOEIC Speaking Test. This test includes eleven questions that measure different aspects of your speaking ability. The test lasts approximately 20 minutes.

Question	Task	Evaluation Criteria
1-2	Read a text aloud	• pronunciation • intonation and stress
3	Describe a picture	all of the above, plus • grammar • vocabulary • cohesion
4-6	Respond to questions	all of the above, plus • relevance of content • completeness of content
7-9	Respond to questions using information provided	all of the above
10	Propose a solution	all of the above
11	Express an opinion	all of the above

For each type of question, you will be given specific directions, including the time allowed for preparation and speaking.

It is to your advantage to say as much as you can in the time allowed. It is also important that you speak clearly and that you answer each question according to the directions.

Click on **Continue** to go on.

Questions 1-2: Read a text aloud

Directions: In this part of the test, you will read aloud the text on the screen. You will have 45 seconds to prepare. Then you will have 45 seconds to read the text aloud.

TOEIC® Speaking

Question 3: Describe a picture

Directions: In this part of the test, you will describe the picture on your screen in as much detail as you can. You will have 30 seconds to prepare your response. Then you will have 45 seconds to speak about the picture.

TOEIC® Speaking

Question 3 of 11

PREPARATION TIME
00:00:30

RESPONSE TIME
00:00:45

TOEIC® Speaking

Question 1 of 11

Hi, this is Annabelle. If you want to leave a message, please wait for the tone. If you want to leave your name and a message, press one, then speak loudly after the beep. If you want to leave your number only, please press two, and enter the number. I will call you back as soon as possible once I come home.

PREPARATION TIME
00:00:45

RESPONSE TIME
00:00:45

TOEIC® Speaking

Question 2 of 11

Today, we will begin our special conference. As all of you know, we have been involved in a very important project since last spring. We finally completed that project last month with great progress. This is our way of saying thank you to all of you. Let me tell you that no one knew about this special session for this morning. Let's give a very big welcome to our partner to celebrate our great performance. This is Ellen Lavigne.

PREPARATION TIME
00:00:45

RESPONSE TIME
00:00:45

Questions 4-6: Respond to questions

Directions: In this part of the test, you will answer three questions. For each question, begin responding immediately after you hear a beep. No preparation time is provided. You will have 15 seconds to respond to Questions 4 and 5 and 30 seconds to respond to Question 6.

Question 4 of 11

Imagine that an American marketing firm is doing research in your country. You have agreed to participate in a telephone interview about a movie.

Have you recently seen any movies in foreign languages?

RESPONSE TIME
00:00:15

Question 5 of 11

Imagine that an American marketing firm is doing research in your country. You have agreed to participate in a telephone interview about a movie.

Where and when do you usually watch foreign movies?

RESPONSE TIME
00:00:15

Question 6 of 11

Imagine that an American marketing firm is doing research in your country. You have agreed to participate in a telephone interview about a movie.

Are you willing to buy a movie ticket to watch a movie starring unknown actors?

RESPONSE TIME
00:00:30

TOEIC® Speaking

Questions 7-9: Respond to questions using information provided

Directions: In this part of the test, you will answer three questions based on the information provided. You will have 30 seconds to read the information before the questions begin. For each question, begin responding immediately after you hear a beep. No additional preparation time is provided. You will have 15 seconds to respond to Questions 7 and 8 and 30 seconds to respond to Question 9.

TOEIC® Speaking

Rolling Stones Music Festival

Conner Valley Hotel, March 4th~7th

Date	Time	Event	Venue
Fri. March 4th	1 p.m.	Opening Ceremony	Seaside Auditorium
Fri. March 4th	5 p.m.	Old Pop Songs from the 70s and 80s Concert* by Woody Court	Circular Auditorium
Sat. March 5th	6 p.m.	Rock Music Concert* by Foreign Indie Bands	Circular Auditorium
Sun. March 6th	6 p.m.	21st Century's Hot Selling Albums' Music Concert*	Seaside Auditorium
Mon. March 7th	4 p.m.	Dance Party with the Best Bands from 2013	B.B. Conference Hall

* All concert tickets include free drinks and snacks but are limited.

PREPARATION TIME
00:00:30

Rolling Stones Music Festival

Conner Valley Hotel, March 4th~7th

Date	Time	Event	Venue
Fri. March 4th	1 p.m.	Opening Ceremony	Seaside Auditorium
Fri. March 4th	5 p.m.	Old Pop Songs from the 70s and 80s Concert* by Woody Court	Circular Auditorium
Sat. March 5th	6 p.m.	Rock Music Concert* by Foreign Indie Bands	Circular Auditorium
Sun. March 6th	6 p.m.	21st Century's Hot Selling Albums' Music Concert*	Seaside Auditorium
Mon. March 7th	4 p.m.	Dance Party with the Best Bands from 2013	B.B. Conference Hall

* All concert tickets include free drinks and snacks but are limited.

RESPONSE TIME
00:00:15

Question 10: Propose a solution

Directions: In this part of the test, you will be presented with a problem and asked to propose a solution. You will have 30 seconds to prepare. Then you will have 60 seconds to speak.

In your response, be sure to
- show that you recognize the problem, and
- propose a way of dealing with the problem.

Rolling Stones Music Festival

Conner Valley Hotel, March 4th~7th

Date	Time	Event	Venue
Fri. March 4th	1 p.m.	Opening Ceremony	Seaside Auditorium
Fri. March 4th	5 p.m.	Old Pop Songs from the 70s and 80s Concert* by Woody Court	Circular Auditorium
Sat. March 5th	6 p.m.	Rock Music Concert* by Foreign Indie Bands	Circular Auditorium
Sun. March 6th	6 p.m.	21st Century's Hot Selling Albums' Music Concert*	Seaside Auditorium
Mon. March 7th	4 p.m.	Dance Party with the Best Bands from 2013	B.B. Conference Hall

* All concert tickets include free drinks and snacks but are limited.

RESPONSE TIME
00:00:30

TOEIC® Speaking

Question 11: Express an opinion

Directions: In this part of the test, you will give your opinion about a specific topic. Be sure to say as much as you can in the time allowed. You will have 15 seconds to prepare. Then you will have 60 seconds to speak.

TOEIC® Speaking

Question 11 of 11

Do you agree or disagree with the following statement?

Companies should compensate their hard workers with sufficient vacation leave.

Use specific reasons or examples to support your opinion.

PREPARATION TIME
00:00:15

RESPONSE TIME
00:01:00

TOEIC® Speaking

Question 10 of 11

TOEIC® Speaking

Question 10 of 11

Respond as if you are the company's Managing Director.

In your response, be sure to
- show that you recognize the problem, and
- propose a way of dealing with the problem.

PREPARATION TIME
00:00:30

RESPONSE TIME
00:01:00

Actual Test 03

TOEIC® Speaking

Speaking Test Directions

This is the TOEIC Speaking Test. This test includes eleven questions that measure different aspects of your speaking ability. The test lasts approximately 20 minutes.

Question	Task	Evaluation Criteria
1-2	Read a text aloud	• pronunciation • intonation and stress
3	Describe a picture	all of the above, plus • grammar • vocabulary • cohesion
4-6	Respond to questions	all of the above, plus • relevance of content • completeness of content
7-9	Respond to questions using information provided	all of the above
10	Propose a solution	all of the above
11	Express an opinion	all of the above

For each type of question, you will be given specific directions, including the time allowed for preparation and speaking.

It is to your advantage to say as much as you can in the time allowed. It is also important that you speak clearly and that you answer each question according to the directions.

Click on **Continue** to go on.

TOEIC® Speaking

Questions 1-2: Read a text aloud

Directions: In this part of the test, you will read aloud the text on the screen. You will have 45 seconds to prepare. Then you will have 45 seconds to read the text aloud.

TOEIC® Speaking

Question 1 of 11

Are you tired of your current career? Are you looking for the job of your life? Do you want to be your own boss? If your answer is "Yes" and you are under 35 years of age with good computer and Internet skills, we will offer you a chance for suitable financing and an unlimited and steady income. Please email your résumé to the following address: golden@job.com.

PREPARATION TIME
00:00:45

RESPONSE TIME
00:00:45

TOEIC® Speaking

Question 2 of 11

This is Wendy in Boston. On highway 191 westbound between junctions J1 and J2, minor delays are possible due to bumper-to-bumper traffic following the closing of one lane. Normal traffic conditions are expected after 8:00 a.m. And on highway 191 eastbound between junctions J9 and J8, there are currently delays of 15 minutes due to a broken down pickup truck. Traffic flow will even out within 1 hour.

PREPARATION TIME
00:00:45

RESPONSE TIME
00:00:45

TOEIC® Speaking

Question 3: Describe a picture

Directions: In this part of the test, you will describe the picture on your screen in as much detail as you can. You will have 30 seconds to prepare your response. Then you will have 45 seconds to speak about the picture.

TOEIC® Speaking

Question 3 of 11

PREPARATION TIME
00:00:30

RESPONSE TIME
00:00:45

TOEIC® Speaking

Questions 4-6: Respond to questions

Directions: In this part of the test, you will answer three questions. For each question, begin responding immediately after you hear a beep. No preparation time is provided. You will have 15 seconds to respond to Questions 4 and 5 and 30 seconds to respond to Question 6.

TOEIC® Speaking Question 4 of 11

Imagine that a British marketing firm is doing research in your country. You have agreed to participate in a telephone interview about cellular phones.

How many text messages do you receive a day?

RESPONSE TIME
00:00:15

TOEIC® Speaking Question 5 of 11

Imagine that a British marketing firm is doing research in your country. You have agreed to participate in a telephone interview about cellular phones.

What kind of service do you use with your cellular phone?

RESPONSE TIME
00:00:15

TOEIC® Speaking Question 6 of 11

Imagine that a British marketing firm is doing research in your country. You have agreed to participate in a telephone interview about cellular phones.

When you contact your friends, do you send a text message or make a phone call?

RESPONSE TIME
00:00:30

TOEIC® Speaking

Questions 7-9: Respond to questions using information provided

Directions: In this part of the test, you will answer three questions based on the information provided. You will have 30 seconds to read the information before the questions begin. For each question, begin responding immediately after you hear a beep. No additional preparation time is provided. You will have 15 seconds to respond to Questions 7 and 8 and 30 seconds to respond to Question 9.

TOEIC® Speaking

New Employee Orientation

August 17th 2013

Main Auditorium, Annex Building of DML Corp.

09:00 a.m. - 09:50 a.m.	Introduction & Welcome Speech, Edward Hamilton, CEO
10:00 a.m. - 10:50 a.m.	"The History of DML Corp." Dr. Rebecca Wilson
11:00 a.m. - 11:50 a.m.	Video Presentation, Erikson Bolt, Education Manager
12:00 p.m. - 01:00 p.m.	Lunch, Edgeware Restaurant
01:00 p.m. - 03:00 p.m.	Group Discussion
03:10 p.m. - 04:00 p.m.	Product Demonstration
04:10 p.m. - 04:50 p.m.	Group Tour of the Factory
05:00 p.m. - 06:00 p.m.	Dinner, Alington Restaurant

PREPARATION TIME

00:00:30

Question 7 of 11

New Employee Orientation

August 17th 2013

Main Auditorium, Annex Building of DML Corp.

Time	Event
09:00 a.m. - 09:50 a.m.	Introduction & Welcome Speech, Edward Hamilton, CEO
10:00 a.m. - 10:50 a.m.	"The History of DML Corp." Dr. Rebecca Wilson
11:00 a.m. - 11:50 a.m.	Video Presentation, Erikson Bolt, Education Manager
12:00 p.m. - 01:00 p.m.	Lunch, Edgeware Restaurant
01:00 p.m. - 03:00 p.m.	Group Discussion
03:10 p.m. - 04:00 p.m.	Product Demonstration
04:10 p.m. - 04:50 p.m.	Group Tour of the Factory
05:00 p.m. - 06:00 p.m.	Dinner, Alington Restaurant

RESPONSE TIME 00:00:15

Question 8 of 11

New Employee Orientation

August 17th 2013

Main Auditorium, Annex Building of DML Corp.

Time	Event
09:00 a.m. - 09:50 a.m.	Introduction & Welcome Speech, Edward Hamilton, CEO
10:00 a.m. - 10:50 a.m.	"The History of DML Corp." Dr. Rebecca Wilson
11:00 a.m. - 11:50 a.m.	Video Presentation, Erikson Bolt, Education Manager
12:00 p.m. - 01:00 p.m.	Lunch, Edgeware Restaurant
01:00 p.m. - 03:00 p.m.	Group Discussion
03:10 p.m. - 04:00 p.m.	Product Demonstration
04:10 p.m. - 04:50 p.m.	Group Tour of the Factory
05:00 p.m. - 06:00 p.m.	Dinner, Alington Restaurant

RESPONSE TIME 00:00:15

Question 10: Propose a solution

Directions: In this part of the test, you will be presented with a problem and asked to propose a solution. You will have 30 seconds to prepare. Then you will have 60 seconds to speak.

In your response, be sure to
- show that you recognize the problem, and
- propose a way of dealing with the problem.

Question 9 of 11

New Employee Orientation

August 17th 2013
Main Auditorium, Annex Building of DML Corp.

09:00 a.m. - 09:50 a.m.	Introduction & Welcome Speech, Edward Hamilton, CEO
10:00 a.m. - 10:50 a.m.	"The History of DML Corp." Dr. Rebecca Wilson
11:00 a.m. - 11:50 a.m.	Video Presentation, Erikson Bolt, Education Manager
12:00 p.m. - 01:00 p.m.	Lunch, Edgeware Restaurant
01:00 p.m. - 03:00 p.m.	Group Discussion
03:10 p.m. - 04:00 p.m.	Product Demonstration
04:10 p.m. - 04:50 p.m.	Group Tour of the Factory
05:00 p.m. - 06:00 p.m.	Dinner, Alington Restaurant

RESPONSE TIME
00:00:30

TOEIC® Speaking

Question 11: Express an opinion

Directions: In this part of the test, you will give your opinion about a specific topic. Be sure to say as much as you can in the time allowed. You will have 15 seconds to prepare. Then you will have 60 seconds to speak.

TOEIC® Speaking

Question 11 of 11

Do you agree or disagree with the following statement?
The government should spend money on building more theaters.
Use specific reasons or examples to support your opinion.

PREPARATION TIME
00:00:15

RESPONSE TIME
00:01:00

TOEIC® Speaking

Question 10 of 11

TOEIC® Speaking

Question 10 of 11

Respond as if you work with Sally.

In your response, be sure to
- show that you recognize the problem, and
- propose a way of dealing with the problem.

PREPARATION TIME
00:00:30

RESPONSE TIME
00:01:00

Actual Test 04

TOEIC® Speaking

Speaking Test Directions

This is the TOEIC Speaking Test. This test includes eleven questions that measure different aspects of your speaking ability. The test lasts approximately 20 minutes.

Question	Task	Evaluation Criteria
1-2	Read a text aloud	• pronunciation • intonation and stress
3	Describe a picture	all of the above, plus • grammar • vocabulary • cohesion
4-6	Respond to questions	all of the above, plus • relevance of content • completeness of content
7-9	Respond to questions using information provided	all of the above
10	Propose a solution	all of the above
11	Express an opinion	all of the above

For each type of question, you will be given specific directions, including the time allowed for preparation and speaking.

It is to your advantage to say as much as you can in the time allowed. It is also important that you speak clearly and that you answer each question according to the directions.

Click on **Continue** to go on.

TOEIC® Speaking

Questions 1-2: Read a text aloud

Directions: In this part of the test, you will read aloud the text on the screen. You will have 45 seconds to prepare. Then you will have 45 seconds to read the text aloud.

TOEIC® Speaking

Question 1 of 11

I'm Phil Davison, your tour guide from Rocky Mountain Tracking. It is a perfect day for hiking. Average temperatures will be around 22℃ and we only have a 5% chance of rain. It will take 3 hours or more to reach the top of the mountain. On the way up, we might have unexpected changes in the weather. Please don't forget to bring your warm clothes.

PREPARATION TIME 00:00:45

RESPONSE TIME 00:00:45

TOEIC® Speaking

Question 2 of 11

Richardson Centre is pleased to announce that it is undergoing an internal renovation in the northwest wing of Stratford Mall. The renovation is expected to begin in early March and it is anticipated that all new and relocated retail stores in that part of the mall will be back in place within about 12 months from the start of renovation.

PREPARATION TIME 00:00:45

RESPONSE TIME 00:00:45

TOEIC® Speaking

Question 3: Describe a picture

Directions: In this part of the test, you will describe the picture on your screen in as much detail as you can. You will have 30 seconds to prepare your response. Then you will have 45 seconds to speak about the picture.

TOEIC® Speaking

Question 3 of 11

PREPARATION TIME 00:00:30

RESPONSE TIME 00:00:45

TOEIC® Speaking

Questions 4-6: Respond to questions

Directions: In this part of the test, you will answer three questions. For each question, begin responding immediately after you hear a beep. No preparation time is provided. You will have 15 seconds to respond to Questions 4 and 5 and 30 seconds to respond to Question 6.

TOEIC® Speaking   Question 4 of 11

Imagine that an Australian marketing firm is doing research in your country. You have agreed to participate in a telephone interview about restaurants.

Which restaurant do you frequently visit to have a meal?

RESPONSE TIME
00:00:15

TOEIC® Speaking   Question 5 of 11

Imagine that an Australian marketing firm is doing research in your country. You have agreed to participate in a telephone interview about restaurants.

When are restaurants in your town crowded with people during any given day?

RESPONSE TIME
00:00:15

TOEIC® Speaking   Question 6 of 11

Imagine that an Australian marketing firm is doing research in your country. You have agreed to participate in a telephone interview about restaurants.

Do you like to try a new restaurant or have a meal in your familiar restaurant?

RESPONSE TIME
00:00:30

TOEIC® Speaking

Questions 7-9: Respond to questions using information provided

Directions: In this part of the test, you will answer three questions based on the information provided. You will have 30 seconds to read the information before the questions begin. For each question, begin responding immediately after you hear a beep. No additional preparation time is provided. You will have 15 seconds to respond to Questions 7 and 8 and 30 seconds to respond to Question 9.

TOEIC® Speaking

Regal Valley Cinema

Session Times Thursday 25th January

Title	Run Time	Show Time			Rate
Extraordinary Measures	1hr 46mins	8:00 a.m.	10:00 a.m.	4:00 p.m.	PG
Legion *new!*	1hr 40mins	7:50 a.m.	11:40 a.m.	6:00 p.m.	R
The Tooth Fairy	1hr 42mins	2:00 p.m.	4:00 p.m.	6:00 p.m.	PG
The Book of Eli	1hr 58mins	11:00 a.m.	3:15 p.m.	5:25 p.m.	R
Sherlock Holmes *new!*	2hrs 14mins	10:00 a.m.	12:50 p.m.	3:30 p.m.	PG-13
Alvin and the Chipmunks	1hr 25mins	9:25 a.m.	3:40 p.m.	5:00 p.m.	PG
Avatar *new!*	2hrs 30mins	7:30 a.m.	10:30 a.m.	2:00 p.m.	PG-13

(PG: Parental Guidance Suggested, PG-13: Some Material Inappropriate for Children Under 13, R: Restricted)

- Child: $6.00, Adult: $9.00, Senior: $6.00
- Child tickets are valid for children 11 years old and under.

PREPARATION TIME
00:00:30

Regal Valley Cinema

Session Times Thursday 25th January

Title	Run Time	Show Time			Rate
Extraordinary Measures	1hr 46mins	8:00 a.m.	10:00 a.m.	4:00 p.m.	PG
Legion *new!*	1hr 40mins	7:50 a.m.	11:40 a.m.	6:00 p.m.	R
The Tooth Fairy	1hr 42mins	2:00 p.m.	4:00 p.m.	6:00 p.m.	PG
The Book of Eli	1hr 58mins	11:00 a.m.	3:15 p.m.	5:25 p.m.	R
Sherlock Holmes *new!*	2hrs 14mins	10:00 a.m.	12:50 p.m.	3:30 p.m.	PG-13
Alvin and the Chipmunks	1hr 25mins	9:25 a.m.	3:40 p.m.	5:00 p.m.	PG
Avatar *new!*	2hrs 30mins	7:30 a.m.	10:30 a.m.	2:00 p.m.	PG-13

(PG: Parental Guidance Suggested, PG-13: Some Material Inappropriate for Children Under 13, R: Restricted)

- Child: $6.00, Adult: $9.00, Senior: $6.00
- Child tickets are valid for children 11 years old and under.

RESPONSE TIME
00:00:15

Question 10: Propose a solution

Directions: In this part of the test, you will be presented with a problem and asked to propose a solution. You will have 30 seconds to prepare. Then you will have 60 seconds to speak.

In your response, be sure to
- show that you recognize the problem, and
- propose a way of dealing with the problem.

Regal Valley Cinema

Session Times Thursday 25th January

Title	Run Time	Show Time			Rate
Extraordinary Measures	1hr 46mins	8:00 a.m.	10:00 a.m.	4:00 p.m.	PG
Legion *new!*	1hr 40mins	7:50 a.m.	11:40 a.m.	6:00 p.m.	R
The Tooth Fairy	1hr 42mins	2:00 p.m.	4:00 p.m.	6:00 p.m.	PG
The Book of Eli	1hr 58mins	11:00 a.m.	3:15 p.m.	5:25 p.m.	R
Sherlock Holmes *new!*	2hrs 14mins	10:00 a.m.	12:50 p.m.	3:30 p.m.	PG-13
Alvin and the Chipmunks	1hr 25mins	9:25 a.m.	3:40 p.m.	5:00 p.m.	PG
Avatar *new!*	2hrs 30mins	7:30 a.m.	10:30 a.m.	2:00 p.m.	PG-13

(PG: Parental Guidance Suggested, PG-13: Some Material Inappropriate for Children Under 13, R: Restricted)

- Child: $6.00, Adult: $9.00, Senior: $6.00
- Child tickets are valid for children 11 years old and under.

RESPONSE TIME
00:00:30

TOEIC® Speaking

Question 10 of 11

TOEIC® Speaking

Question 10 of 11

In your response, be sure to
- show that you recognize the problem, and
- propose a way of dealing with the problem.

PREPARATION TIME
00:00:30

RESPONSE TIME
00:01:00

TOEIC® Speaking

Question 11: Express an opinion

Directions: In this part of the test, you will give your opinion about a specific topic. Be sure to say as much as you can in the time allowed. You will have 15 seconds to prepare. Then you will have 60 seconds to speak.

TOEIC® Speaking

Question 11 of 11

What is the most important factor an employee should have for work success? Choose one of the following options and give specific reasons or examples to support your opinion.

- A sense of humor
- Good looks
- Responsibility

PREPARATION TIME
00:00:15

RESPONSE TIME
00:01:00

Actual Test 05

TOEIC® Speaking

05_01~11

MP3 바로 듣기

Speaking Test Directions

This is the TOEIC Speaking Test. This test includes eleven questions that measure different aspects of your speaking ability. The test lasts approximately 20 minutes.

Question	Task	Evaluation Criteria
1-2	Read a text aloud	• pronunciation • intonation and stress
3	Describe a picture	all of the above, plus • grammar • vocabulary • cohesion
4-6	Respond to questions	all of the above, plus • relevance of content • completeness of content
7-9	Respond to questions using information provided	all of the above
10	Propose a solution	all of the above
11	Express an opinion	all of the above

For each type of question, you will be given specific directions, including the time allowed for preparation and speaking.

It is to your advantage to say as much as you can in the time allowed. It is also important that you speak clearly and that you answer each question according to the directions.

Click on **Continue** to go on.

→ 정답 P23

TOEIC® Speaking

Questions 1-2: Read a text aloud

Directions: In this part of the test, you will read aloud the text on the screen. You will have 45 seconds to prepare. Then you will have 45 seconds to read the text aloud.

TOEIC® Speaking

Question 1 of 11

According to recent research, scientists at University of Mississippi have discovered one reason that obese people eat more than they need. Ericka Myers of the Mississippi Research Institute said, "That is because they have gotten used to overeating and being sedentary. To change this eating habit, they should start their day with a workout."

PREPARATION TIME
00:00:45

RESPONSE TIME
00:00:45

TOEIC® Speaking

Question 2 of 11

The great musicians use various brands of pianos for public concerts before a variety of audiences. However, you will notice that those who care most for their professional reputations usually select the brand Caldwell. The Caldwell Concert Grand piano has gained its prestige in the musical world because artists have found it essential for their best performances. For your own studios and recitals, Caldwell is the perfect choice.

PREPARATION TIME
00:00:45

RESPONSE TIME
00:00:45

TOEIC® Speaking

Question 3: Describe a picture

Directions: In this part of the test, you will describe the picture on your screen in as much detail as you can. You will have 30 seconds to prepare your response. Then you will have 45 seconds to speak about the picture.

TOEIC® Speaking

Question 3 of 11

PREPARATION TIME
00:00:30

RESPONSE TIME
00:00:45

TOEIC® Speaking

Questions 4-6: Respond to questions

Directions: In this part of the test, you will answer three questions. For each question, begin responding immediately after you hear a beep. No preparation time is provided. You will have 15 seconds to respond to Questions 4 and 5 and 30 seconds to respond to Question 6.

TOEIC® Speaking — **Question 4 of 11**

Imagine that a British marketing firm is doing research in your country. You have agreed to participate in a telephone interview about neighbors.

What do you usually do with your neighbors?

RESPONSE TIME
00:00:15

TOEIC® Speaking — **Question 5 of 11**

Imagine that a British marketing firm is doing research in your country. You have agreed to participate in a telephone interview about neighbors.

Where is a good place for you and your neighbors to meet together?

RESPONSE TIME
00:00:15

TOEIC® Speaking — **Question 6 of 11**

Imagine that a British marketing firm is doing research in your country. You have agreed to participate in a telephone interview about neighbors.

What is a good point about your neighbors or your town?

RESPONSE TIME
00:00:30

TOEIC® Speaking

INVOICE
04/15/2013

NAME: Robert Stewart **ADDRESS:** 3928 Nashville Drive **PHONE:** 930-232-5322
CITY: Nashville, TN **ZIP:** 24432

Quantity	Part No.	Description	Price($)	Amount($)
2	14722	BULBS (10/BOX)	0.50	1.00
1	23455	CUTTER	5.65	5.65
1	12670	IMPELLER	19.35	19.35
1		1 HOUR LABOR ($50/hr)	50.00	50.00

SUBTOTAL	76.00
SALES TAX	1.56
TOTAL AMOUNT	77.56

- *REPLACED IMPELLER*
- *EVERYTHING LOOKS GREAT*

- NO RETURNS - on special orders
  - on electrical parts
  - without receipt
  - after 30 days

PREPARATION TIME

00:00:30

TOEIC® Speaking

Questions 7-9: Respond to questions using information provided

Directions: In this part of the test, you will answer three questions based on the information provided. You will have 30 seconds to read the information before the questions begin. For each question, begin responding immediately after you hear a beep. No additional preparation time is provided. You will have 15 seconds to respond to Questions 7 and 8 and 30 seconds to respond to Question 9.

Question 7 of 11

INVOICE
04/15/2013

NAME: Robert Stewart **ADDRESS:** 3928 Nashville Drive **PHONE:** 930-232-5322
CITY: Nashville, TN **ZIP:** 24432

Quantity	Part No.	Description	Price($)	Amount($)
2	14722	BULBS (10/BOX)	0.50	1.00
1	23455	CUTTER	5.65	5.65
1	12670	IMPELLER	19.35	19.35
1		1 HOUR LABOR ($50/hr)	50.00	50.00
			SUBTOTAL	76.00
			SALES TAX	1.56
			TOTAL AMOUNT	77.56

- *REPLACED IMPELLER*
- *EVERYTHING LOOKS GREAT*

- NO RETURNS - on special orders
  - on electrical parts
  - without receipt
  - after 30 days

RESPONSE TIME
00:00:15

Question 8 of 11

INVOICE
04/15/2013

NAME: Robert Stewart **ADDRESS:** 3928 Nashville Drive **PHONE:** 930-232-5322
CITY: Nashville, TN **ZIP:** 24432

Quantity	Part No.	Description	Price($)	Amount($)
2	14722	BULBS (10/BOX)	0.50	1.00
1	23455	CUTTER	5.65	5.65
1	12670	IMPELLER	19.35	19.35
1		1 HOUR LABOR ($50/hr)	50.00	50.00
			SUBTOTAL	76.00
			SALES TAX	1.56
			TOTAL AMOUNT	77.56

- *REPLACED IMPELLER*
- *EVERYTHING LOOKS GREAT*

- NO RETURNS - on special orders
  - on electrical parts
  - without receipt
  - after 30 days

RESPONSE TIME
00:00:15

Question 10: Propose a solution

Directions: In this part of the test, you will be presented with a problem and asked to propose a solution. You will have 30 seconds to prepare. Then you will have 60 seconds to speak.

In your response, be sure to
- show that you recognize the problem, and
- propose a way of dealing with the problem.

INVOICE
04/15/2013

NAME: Robert Stewart   **ADDRESS:** 3928 Nashville Drive   **PHONE:** 930-232-5322
CITY: Nashville, TN   **ZIP:** 24432

Quantity	Part No.	Description	Price($)	Amount($)
2	14722	BULBS (10/BOX)	0.50	1.00
1	23455	CUTTER	5.65	5.65
1	12670	IMPELLER	19.35	19.35
1		1 HOUR LABOR ($50/hr)	50.00	50.00
			SUBTOTAL	76.00
			SALES TAX	1.56
			TOTAL AMOUNT	77.56

- *REPLACED IMPELLER*
- *EVERYTHING LOOKS GREAT*

- NO RETURNS - on special orders
  - on electrical parts
  - without receipt
  - after 30 days

RESPONSE TIME
00:00:30

TOEIC® Speaking

Question 11: Express an opinion

Directions: In this part of the test, you will give your opinion about a specific topic. Be sure to say as much as you can in the time allowed. You will have 15 seconds to prepare. Then you will have 60 seconds to speak.

TOEIC® Speaking

Question 11 of 11

Do you agree or disagree with this statement?
A lot of people have much more interest in their health than in the past.
Please support your opinion with reasons or examples.

PREPARATION TIME
00:00:15

RESPONSE TIME
00:01:00

TOEIC® Speaking

Question 10 of 11

TOEIC® Speaking

Question 10 of 11

In your response, be sure to
- show that you recognize the problem, and
- propose a way of dealing with the problem.

PREPARATION TIME
00:00:30

RESPONSE TIME
00:01:00

Actual Test 06

TOEIC® Speaking

Speaking Test Directions

This is the TOEIC Speaking Test. This test includes eleven questions that measure different aspects of your speaking ability. The test lasts approximately 20 minutes.

Question	Task	Evaluation Criteria
1-2	Read a text aloud	• pronunciation • intonation and stress
3	Describe a picture	all of the above, plus • grammar • vocabulary • cohesion
4-6	Respond to questions	all of the above, plus • relevance of content • completeness of content
7-9	Respond to questions using information provided	all of the above
10	Propose a solution	all of the above
11	Express an opinion	all of the above

For each type of question, you will be given specific directions, including the time allowed for preparation and speaking.

It is to your advantage to say as much as you can in the time allowed. It is also important that you speak clearly and that you answer each question according to the directions.

Click on **Continue** to go on.

TOEIC® Speaking

Questions 1-2: Read a text aloud

Directions: In this part of the test, you will read aloud the text on the screen. You will have 45 seconds to prepare. Then you will have 45 seconds to read the text aloud.

TOEIC® Speaking

Question 1 of 11

Are you looking for hotels for your next trip? Please visit worldhotel.com without hesitation. Our 2013 New Year's special event is in progress now. We offer free breakfast vouchers to parents with children on their vacations. If three or more families book a room, an extra bed will be provided free of charge. Thanks to our agreements with the world's finest hotels, you will be able to experience the best service. If you want additional information, please call us at 070-123-1234.

PREPARATION TIME
00:00:45

RESPONSE TIME
00:00:45

TOEIC® Speaking

Question 2 of 11

Hello, I will provide you with the 57-minute weather forecast now from RFM radio station. Across the province, lots of rain today. From the southern part of peninsula, we will have strong winds and rain. From the afternoon onwards, it should gradually clear up. Please do not forget to bring your umbrella on the way to work this morning. Today, the average temperature will be 21℃, which is lower than in previous years. The high is 24℃, the low is 13℃. This is Robin Castaneda of RFM radio station.

PREPARATION TIME
00:00:45

RESPONSE TIME
00:00:45

TOEIC® Speaking

Question 3: Describe a picture

Directions: In this part of the test, you will describe the picture on your screen in as much detail as you can. You will have 30 seconds to prepare your response. Then you will have 45 seconds to speak about the picture.

TOEIC® Speaking

Question 3 of 11

PREPARATION TIME
00:00:30

RESPONSE TIME
00:00:45

TOEIC® Speaking

Questions 4-6: Respond to questions

Directions: In this part of the test, you will answer three questions. For each question, begin responding immediately after you hear a beep. No preparation time is provided. You will have 15 seconds to respond to Questions 4 and 5 and 30 seconds to respond to Question 6.

TOEIC® Speaking — **Question 4 of 11**

Imagine that a Canadian marketing firm is doing research in your country. You have agreed to participate in a telephone interview about sweets and candies.

How often do you grab a bite of sweets or candies?

RESPONSE TIME
00:00:15

TOEIC® Speaking — **Question 5 of 11**

Imagine that a Canadian marketing firm is doing research in your country. You have agreed to participate in a telephone interview about sweets and candies.

What are some popular sweets or candies in your country?

RESPONSE TIME
00:00:15

TOEIC® Speaking — **Question 6 of 11**

Imagine that a Canadian marketing firm is doing research in your country. You have agreed to participate in a telephone interview about sweets and candies.

What do you consider when you pick candies up in a store?

RESPONSE TIME
00:00:30

TOEIC® Speaking

Questions 7-9: Respond to questions using information provided

Directions: In this part of the test, you will answer three questions based on the information provided. You will have 30 seconds to read the information before the questions begin. For each question, begin responding immediately after you hear a beep. No additional preparation time is provided. You will have 15 seconds to respond to Questions 7 and 8 and 30 seconds to respond to Question 9.

TOEIC® Speaking

UNIQUE CONSTRUCTION AGENCY WORKSHOP

Friday, July 14th
Main Building, Meeting Room C

Time	Session	Speaker
9:00~9:50	Safety education	Christopher Nolan
10:00~11:50	Demonstration: How to Use Protective Gear–Gloves, Safety Vests	Jay Porter
12:00~1:00	Lunch (Cafeteria)	
1:00~1:50	Presentation: How to Read Blue Prints	Kale Hong
2:00~2:50	Video clips: Wonders about the Construction Site	Roid Gamadon
3:00~3:50	Practice: Visit the construction site	

• After the workshop, all attendees must assist with cleanup at the construction site.

PREPARATION TIME
00:00:30

UNIQUE CONSTRUCTION AGENCY WORKSHOP

Friday, July 14th
Main Building, Meeting Room C

Time	Session	Speaker
9:00~9:50	Safety education	Christopher Nolan
10:00~11:50	Demonstration: How to Use Protective Gear—Gloves, Safety Vests	Jay Porter
12:00~1:00	Lunch (Cafeteria)	
1:00~1:50	Presentation: How to Read Blue Prints	Kale Hong
2:00~2:50	Video clips: Wonders about the Construction Site	Roid Gamadon
3:00~3:50	Practice: Visit the construction site	

- After the workshop, all attendees must assist with cleanup at the construction site.

RESPONSE TIME
00:00:15

UNIQUE CONSTRUCTION AGENCY WORKSHOP

Friday, July 14th
Main Building, Meeting Room C

Time	Session	Speaker
9:00~9:50	Safety education	Christopher Nolan
10:00~11:50	Demonstration: How to Use Protective Gear—Gloves, Safety Vests	Jay Porter
12:00~1:00	Lunch (Cafeteria)	
1:00~1:50	Presentation: How to Read Blue Prints	Kale Hong
2:00~2:50	Video clips: Wonders about the Construction Site	Roid Gamadon
3:00~3:50	Practice: Visit the construction site	

- After the workshop, all attendees must assist with cleanup at the construction site.

RESPONSE TIME
00:00:15

Question 9 of 11

UNIQUE CONSTRUCTION AGENCY WORKSHOP

Friday, July 14th
Main Building, Meeting Room C

Time	Session	Speaker
9:00~9:50	Safety education	Christopher Nolan
10:00~11:50	Demonstration: How to Use Protective Gear—Gloves, Safety Vests	Jay Porter
12:00~1:00	Lunch (Cafeteria)	
1:00~1:50	Presentation: How to Read Blue Prints	Kale Hong
2:00~2:50	Video clips: Wonders about the Construction Site	Roid Gamadon
3:00~3:50	Practice: Visit the construction site	

• After the workshop, all attendees must assist with cleanup at the construction site.

RESPONSE TIME
00:00:30

Question 10: Propose a solution

Directions: In this part of the test, you will be presented with a problem and asked to propose a solution. You will have 30 seconds to prepare. Then you will have 60 seconds to speak.

In your response, be sure to
- show that you recognize the problem, and
- propose a way of dealing with the problem.

TOEIC® Speaking

Question 11: Express an opinion

Directions: In this part of the test, you will give your opinion about a specific topic. Be sure to say as much as you can in the time allowed. You will have 15 seconds to prepare. Then you will have 60 seconds to speak.

TOEIC® Speaking

Question 11 of 11

Do you agree or disagree with this statement?
Some people say that we should invest in developing alternative energy sources to replace unrenewable ones like fossil fuel.
Please support your opinion with reasons or examples.

PREPARATION TIME
00:00:15

RESPONSE TIME
00:01:00

TOEIC® Speaking

Question 10 of 11

TOEIC® Speaking

Question 10 of 11

In your response, be sure to
- show that you recognize the problem, and
- propose a way of dealing with the problem.

PREPARATION TIME
00:00:30

RESPONSE TIME
00:01:00

Actual Test 07

TOEIC® Speaking

Speaking Test Directions

This is the TOEIC Speaking Test. This test includes eleven questions that measure different aspects of your speaking ability. The test lasts approximately 20 minutes.

Question	Task	Evaluation Criteria
1-2	Read a text aloud	• pronunciation • intonation and stress
3	Describe a picture	all of the above, plus • grammar • vocabulary • cohesion
4-6	Respond to questions	all of the above, plus • relevance of content • completeness of content
7-9	Respond to questions using information provided	all of the above
10	Propose a solution	all of the above
11	Express an opinion	all of the above

For each type of question, you will be given specific directions, including the time allowed for preparation and speaking.

It is to your advantage to say as much as you can in the time allowed. It is also important that you speak clearly and that you answer each question according to the directions.

Click on **Continue** to go on.

TOEIC® Speaking

Questions 1-2: Read a text aloud

Directions: In this part of the test, you will read aloud the text on the screen. You will have 45 seconds to prepare. Then you will have 45 seconds to read the text aloud.

TOEIC® Speaking

Question 1 of 11

Welcome to the Gley Co. Repair Service Center. Depending on your specific needs, you may dial and can be connected to one of our agents. Please press 1 for the repair of home appliances, press 2 for the repair of computers and computer peripherals. Please press the # button for other counseling needs. If you want to have personal consultation, please leave your phone number after dialing the * button. Once we get your phone call, we will get back to you.

PREPARATION TIME
00:00:45

RESPONSE TIME
00:00:45

TOEIC® Speaking

Question 2 of 11

Now we will start boarding JF 304 bound for Jeju. This flight is scheduled to take off at 10:35. Please come to gate L14. The elderly and first class passengers will board first followed by prestige, business, and economy class in that order. Please have ready your luggage, passport and flight ticket. Please show your passport and boarding pass to our staff in front of the gate.

PREPARATION TIME
00:00:45

RESPONSE TIME
00:00:45

TOEIC® Speaking

Question 3: Describe a picture

Directions: In this part of the test, you will describe the picture on your screen in as much detail as you can. You will have 30 seconds to prepare your response. Then you will have 45 seconds to speak about the picture.

TOEIC® Speaking

Question 3 of 11

PREPARATION TIME
00:00:30

RESPONSE TIME
00:00:45

Questions 4-6: Respond to questions

Directions: In this part of the test, you will answer three questions. For each question, begin responding immediately after you hear a beep. No preparation time is provided. You will have 15 seconds to respond to Questions 4 and 5 and 30 seconds to respond to Question 6.

Question 4 of 11

Imagine that an Australian marketing firm is doing research in your country. You have agreed to participate in a telephone interview about museums.

What kinds of museum are you interested in?

RESPONSE TIME
00:00:15

Question 5 of 11

Imagine that an Australian marketing firm is doing research in your country. You have agreed to participate in a telephone interview about museums.

Where can you go for the most exotic museums?

RESPONSE TIME
00:00:15

Question 6 of 11

Imagine that an Australian marketing firm is doing research in your country. You have agreed to participate in a telephone interview about museums.

When you choose a museum, which do you consider?

- Theme
- Distance
- History

RESPONSE TIME
00:00:30

Questions 7-9: Respond to questions using information provided

Directions: In this part of the test, you will answer three questions based on the information provided. You will have 30 seconds to read the information before the questions begin. For each question, begin responding immediately after you hear a beep. No additional preparation time is provided. You will have 15 seconds to respond to Questions 7 and 8 and 30 seconds to respond to Question 9.

Interview Schedule for Restart Company

Monday, 8th September, 2013

Department	Interviewer	Applicant	Time	Venue
Marketing	Marketing Manager	Mike Timber	11:00 a.m.	Interview Room A
	CEO	Jackson Call	3:30 p.m.	Executive Room B
Accounting	CFO	Kelly White	2:30 p.m.	Executive Room A
	Accounting Assistant Manager	Steve Runner	11:30 a.m.	Interview Room B
Recruiting*	Recruiting Manager	Claire Golden	11:00 a.m.	Interview Room C
	CEO	Porter Carter	4:30 p.m.	Executive Room A

* The Recruiting Department interviews will last approximately 30 minutes.

PREPARATION TIME
00:00:30

Interview Schedule for Restart Company

Monday, 8th September, 2013

Department	Interviewer	Applicant	Time	Venue
Marketing	Marketing Manager	Mike Timber	11:00 a.m.	Interview Room A
	CEO	Jackson Call	3:30 p.m.	Executive Room B
Accounting	CFO	Kelly White	2:30 p.m.	Executive Room A
	Accounting Assistant Manager	Steve Runner	11:30 a.m.	Interview Room B
Recruiting*	Recruiting Manager	Claire Golden	11:00 a.m.	Interview Room C
	CEO	Porter Carter	4:30 p.m.	Executive Room A

* The Recruiting Department interviews will last approximately 30 minutes.

RESPONSE TIME 00:00:15

Question 10: Propose a solution

Directions: In this part of the test, you will be presented with a problem and asked to propose a solution. You will have 30 seconds to prepare. Then you will have 60 seconds to speak.

In your response, be sure to
- show that you recognize the problem, and
- propose a way of dealing with the problem.

Interview Schedule for Restart Company

Monday, 8th September, 2013

Department	Interviewer	Applicant	Time	Venue
Marketing	Marketing Manager	Mike Timber	11:00 a.m.	Interview Room A
	CEO	Jackson Call	3:30 p.m.	Executive Room B
	CFO	Kelly White	2:30 p.m.	Executive Room A
Accounting	Accounting Assistant Manager	Steve Runner	11:30 a.m.	Interview Room B
Recruiting*	Recruiting Manager	Claire Golden	11:00 a.m.	Interview Room C
	CEO	Porter Carter	4:30 p.m.	Executive Room A

* The Recruiting Department interviews will last approximately 30 minutes.

RESPONSE TIME
00:00:30

TOEIC® Speaking

Question 11: Express an opinion

Directions: In this part of the test, you will give your opinion about a specific topic. Be sure to say as much as you can in the time allowed. You will have 15 seconds to prepare. Then you will have 60 seconds to speak.

TOEIC® Speaking

Question 11 of 11

Do you agree or disagree with this statement?

These days more and more companies have lots of interests in holding on to their regular customers rather than attracting new customers.

Please support your opinion with reasons or examples.

PREPARATION TIME
00:00:15

RESPONSE TIME
00:01:00

TOEIC® Speaking

Question 10 of 11

TOEIC® Speaking

Question 10 of 11

In your response, be sure to
- show that you recognize the problem, and
- propose a way of dealing with the problem.

PREPARATION TIME
00:00:30

RESPONSE TIME
00:01:00

Actual Test 08

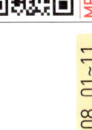

Speaking Test Directions

This is the TOEIC Speaking Test. This test includes eleven questions that measure different aspects of your speaking ability. The test lasts approximately 20 minutes.

Question	Task	Evaluation Criteria
1-2	Read a text aloud	• pronunciation • intonation and stress
3	Describe a picture	all of the above, plus • grammar • vocabulary • cohesion
4-6	Respond to questions	all of the above, plus • relevance of content • completeness of content
7-9	Respond to questions using information provided	all of the above
10	Propose a solution	all of the above
11	Express an opinion	all of the above

For each type of question, you will be given specific directions, including the time allowed for preparation and speaking.

It is to your advantage to say as much as you can in the time allowed. It is also important that you speak clearly and that you answer each question according to the directions.

Click on **Continue** to go on.

Questions 1-2: Read a text aloud

Directions: In this part of the test, you will read aloud the text on the screen. You will have 45 seconds to prepare. Then you will have 45 seconds to read the text aloud.

TOEIC® Speaking

Question 1 of 11

A great gift and accessory store in Evanston and Lake Geneva! We feature rare and limited items for you to browse in our special collection. You can find these products and much more in our stores. Everything in our store can be purchased through the Internet. And then they will be delivered to all over the world. You can enjoy your day right here. If you can't find what you are looking for, please send an email at accessories@gmail.com and we will help you out.

PREPARATION TIME
00:00:45

RESPONSE TIME
00:00:45

TOEIC® Speaking

Question 2 of 11

This is your tour guide Jackson. If you'd like to visit the Vatican Museums without the long entrance queues, please book a one-day pass with us on our website in advance. The pre-paid tickets can include both the entrance fee and lunch passes. After skipping the line, you can explore the Vatican Museums with a tour guide. At the end of the tour, you may stop by the souvenir shops. You can purchase any item at a 30% discount rate. Please just show your one-day pass to the cashier. Thank you.

PREPARATION TIME
00:00:45

RESPONSE TIME
00:00:45

TOEIC® Speaking

Question 3: Describe a picture

Directions: In this part of the test, you will describe the picture on your screen in as much detail as you can. You will have 30 seconds to prepare your response. Then you will have 45 seconds to speak about the picture.

TOEIC® Speaking

Question 3 of 11

PREPARATION TIME
00:00:30

RESPONSE TIME
00:00:45

TOEIC® Speaking

Questions 4-6: Respond to questions

Directions: In this part of the test, you will answer three questions. For each question, begin responding immediately after you hear a beep. No preparation time is provided. You will have 15 seconds to respond to Questions 4 and 5 and 30 seconds to respond to Question 6.

TOEIC® Speaking — Question 4 of 11

Imagine that an American marketing firm is doing research in your country. You have agreed to participate in a telephone interview about taking photos.

How often and with what devices do you take a photo?

RESPONSE TIME
00:00:15

TOEIC® Speaking — Question 5 of 11

Imagine that an American marketing firm is doing research in your country. You have agreed to participate in a telephone interview about taking photos.

Where do you usually store your photos?

RESPONSE TIME
00:00:15

TOEIC® Speaking — Question 6 of 11

Imagine that an American marketing firm is doing research in your country. You have agreed to participate in a telephone interview about taking photos.

Are you willing to pay for someone to arrange your pictures instead of you?

RESPONSE TIME
00:00:30

TOEIC® Speaking

Questions 7-9: Respond to questions using information provided

Directions: In this part of the test, you will answer three questions based on the information provided. You will have 30 seconds to read the information before the questions begin. For each question, begin responding immediately after you hear a beep. No additional preparation time is provided. You will have 15 seconds to respond to Questions 7 and 8 and 30 seconds to respond to Question 9.

TOEIC® Speaking

Best Seat Travel Agency

Kongka Inc. 523 Wiky Street Indianapolis, IN 45216
Phone (241) 214-8973

Emailed: November 29, 2013
Jimmy Banks' Itinerary

Date	Flight No.	Departure time	Departure from	Arrival at
December 20	Air Paris KL 430	7:30 a.m.	Paris	Seoul
December 22	Air Seoul JL 254	8:10 a.m.	Seoul	Brasilia
December 24	Alpha PL 678	9:00 a.m.	Brasilia	New York
December 27	Alpha CP 315	5:00 p.m.	New York	Paris

• Change your itinerary at least 2 days before departure by calling at (201) 348-3476. (Ext. 230)

PREPARATION TIME
00:00:30

Best Seat Travel Agency

Kongka Inc. 523 Wiky Street Indianapolis, IN 45216
Phone (241) 214-8973

Emailed: November 29, 2013
Jimmy Banks' Itinerary

Date	Flight No.	Departure time	Departure from	Arrival at
December 20	Air Paris KL 430	7:30 a.m.	Paris	Seoul
December 22	Air Seoul JL 254	8:10 a.m.	Seoul	Brasilia
December 24	Alpha PL 678	9:00 a.m.	Brasilia	New York
December 27	Alpha CP 315	5:00 p.m.	New York	Paris

- Change your itinerary at least 2 days before departure by calling at (201) 348-3476. (Ext. 230)

RESPONSE TIME 00:00:15

TOEIC® Speaking

Question 10: Propose a solution

Directions: In this part of the test, you will be presented with a problem and asked to propose a solution. You will have 30 seconds to prepare. Then you will have 60 seconds to speak.

In your response, be sure to
- show that you recognize the problem, and
- propose a way of dealing with the problem.

TOEIC® Speaking — Question 9 of 11

Best Seat Travel Agency

Kongka Inc. 523 Wiky Street Indianapolis, IN 45216
Phone (241) 214-8973

Emailed: November 29, 2013
Jimmy Banks' Itinerary

Date	Flight No.	Departure time	Departure from	Arrival at
December 20	Air Paris KL 430	7:30 a.m.	Paris	Seoul
December 22	Air Seoul JL 254	8:10 a.m.	Seoul	Brasilia
December 24	Alpha PL 678	9:00 a.m.	Brasilia	New York
December 27	Alpha CP 315	5:00 p.m.	New York	Paris

• Change your itinerary at least 2 days before departure by calling at (201) 348-3476. (Ext. 230)

RESPONSE TIME
00:00:30

Question 11: Express an opinion

Directions: In this part of the test, you will give your opinion about a specific topic. Be sure to say as much as you can in the time allowed. You will have 15 seconds to prepare. Then you will have 60 seconds to speak.

Question 11 of 11

Do you agree that a job interview is the best way to hire suitable workers for a company? Why or why not? Use specific reasons or examples to support your opinion.

PREPARATION TIME
00:00:15

RESPONSE TIME
00:01:00

Question 10 of 11

Question 10 of 11

In your response, be sure to
- show that you recognize the problem, and
- propose a way of dealing with the problem.

PREPARATION TIME
00:00:30

RESPONSE TIME
00:01:00

Actual Test 09

TOEIC® Speaking

Speaking Test Directions

This is the TOEIC Speaking Test. This test includes eleven questions that measure different aspects of your speaking ability. The test lasts approximately 20 minutes.

Question	Task	Evaluation Criteria
1-2	Read a text aloud	• pronunciation • intonation and stress
3	Describe a picture	all of the above, plus • grammar • vocabulary • cohesion
4-6	Respond to questions	all of the above, plus • relevance of content • completeness of content
7-9	Respond to questions using information provided	all of the above
10	Propose a solution	all of the above
11	Express an opinion	all of the above

For each type of question, you will be given specific directions, including the time allowed for preparation and speaking.

It is to your advantage to say as much as you can in the time allowed. It is also important that you speak clearly and that you answer each question according to the directions.

Click on **Continue** to go on.

TOEIC® Speaking

Questions 1-2: Read a text aloud

Directions: In this part of the test, you will read aloud the text on the screen. You will have 45 seconds to prepare. Then you will have 45 seconds to read the text aloud.

TOEIC® Speaking   **Question 1 of 11**

Build Your Muscles Gym is the perfect place for the entire family, from grandchildren to grandparents. If you register with us before March, you can buy our membership for only $50. It includes training suits, gymnasium shoes and one locker. After March 1st, registration is up to $70. Children under 15 can get a membership for only $20. All members will receive free parking tickets, one free personal training program and group exercise classes. Why don't you build your muscles right here with us?

PREPARATION TIME
00:00:45

RESPONSE TIME
00:00:45

TOEIC® Speaking   **Question 2 of 11**

Welcome to Real Story. As we advertised before, today we have a very special guest. The youngest person with a Harvard Ph.D. degree in our country, who was also designated the first female minister, is here with us today. She has published a number of books that have inspired teenagers and students experiencing the challenges of adolescence. Today, we will listen to her personal history. Please give a huge round of applause and a big welcome to Catherine Flower, former Minister of Education.

PREPARATION TIME
00:00:45

RESPONSE TIME
00:00:45

TOEIC® Speaking   **Question 3: Describe a picture**

Directions: In this part of the test, you will describe the picture on your screen in as much detail as you can. You will have 30 seconds to prepare your response. Then you will have 45 seconds to speak about the picture.

TOEIC® Speaking   **Question 3 of 11**

PREPARATION TIME
00:00:30

RESPONSE TIME
00:00:45

TOEIC® Speaking

Questions 4-6: Respond to questions

Directions: In this part of the test, you will answer three questions. For each question, begin responding immediately after you hear a beep. No preparation time is provided. You will have 15 seconds to respond to Questions 4 and 5 and 30 seconds to respond to Question 6.

TOEIC® Speaking **Question 4 of 11**

Imagine that a British marketing firm is doing research in your country. You have agreed to participate in a telephone interview about public transportation.

When do you usually use public transportation?

RESPONSE TIME
00:00:15

TOEIC® Speaking **Question 5 of 11**

Imagine that a British marketing firm is doing research in your country. You have agreed to participate in a telephone interview about public transportation.

What is your favorite form of public transportation?

RESPONSE TIME
00:00:15

TOEIC® Speaking **Question 6 of 11**

Imagine that a British marketing firm is doing research in your country. You have agreed to participate in a telephone interview about public c transportation.

Please tell me how you got here this morning in detail.

RESPONSE TIME
00:00:30

TOEIC® Speaking

Questions 7-9: Respond to questions using information provided

Directions: In this part of the test, you will answer three questions based on the information provided. You will have 30 seconds to read the information before the questions begin. For each question, begin responding immediately after you hear a beep. No additional preparation time is provided. You will have 15 seconds to respond to Questions 7 and 8 and 30 seconds to respond to Question 9.

TOEIC® Speaking

Willington Community Center Summer Program

August, 2013

Days	Classes	Times	Locations	Target
Monday	Swimming	7:00 a.m. 8:00 a.m.	Swimming pool	Basic courses for beginners
Tuesday	Aerobics	7:00 a.m. 7:00 p.m.	Multipurpose hall	For those under 50 years old
Wednesday	Marathon	6:00 a.m.	Myers Park	Marathon prep courses
Thursday	Tennis	7:00 a.m. 7:00 p.m.	Tennis court	Practice matches for advanced learners
Friday	Yoga	7:00 a.m. 7:00 p.m.	Multipurpose hall	All age groups

- All classes start on the first day of every month. Please register at least one day before the first day of class.

PREPARATION TIME
00:00:30

Willington Community Center Summer Program

August, 2013

Days	Classes	Times	Locations	Target
Monday	Swimming	7:00 a.m. 8:00 a.m.	Swimming pool	Basic courses for beginners
Tuesday	Aerobics	7:00 a.m. 7:00 p.m.	Multipurpose hall	For those under 50 years old
Wednesday	Marathon	6:00 a.m.	Myers Park	Marathon prep courses
Thursday	Tennis	7:00 a.m. 7:00 p.m.	Tennis court	Practice matches for advanced learners
Friday	Yoga	7:00 a.m. 7:00 p.m.	Multipurpose hall	All age groups

- All classes start on the first day of every month. Please register at least one day before the first day of class.

RESPONSE TIME 00:00:15

Question 10: Propose a solution

Directions: In this part of the test, you will be presented with a problem and asked to propose a solution. You will have 30 seconds to prepare. Then you will have 60 seconds to speak.

In your response, be sure to
- show that you recognize the problem, and
- propose a way of dealing with the problem.

Willington Community Center Summer Program

August, 2013

Days	Classes	Times	Locations	Target
Monday	Swimming	7:00 a.m. 8:00 a.m.	Swimming pool	Basic courses for beginners
Tuesday	Aerobics	7:00 a.m. 7:00 p.m.	Multipurpose hall	For those under 50 years old
Wednesday	Marathon	6:00 a.m.	Myers Park	Marathon prep courses
Thursday	Tennis	7:00 a.m. 7:00 p.m.	Tennis court	Practice matches for advanced learners
Friday	Yoga	7:00 a.m. 7:00 p.m.	Multipurpose hall	All age groups

- All classes start on the first day of every month. Please register at least one day before the first day of class.

RESPONSE TIME
00:00:30

TOEIC® Speaking

Question 11: Express an opinion

Directions: In this part of the test, you will give your opinion about a specific topic. Be sure to say as much as you can in the time allowed. You will have 15 seconds to prepare. Then you will have 60 seconds to speak.

TOEIC® Speaking

Question 11 of 11

Who do you think is the most important category of people? Please choose one among the following and support your opinion with reasons or examples.

- Politicians
- Scientists
- Teachers

PREPARATION TIME
00:00:15

RESPONSE TIME
00:01:00

TOEIC® Speaking

Question 10 of 11

TOEIC® Speaking

Question 10 of 11

In your response, be sure to
- show that you recognize the problem, and
- propose a way of dealing with the problem.

PREPARATION TIME
00:00:30

RESPONSE TIME
00:01:00

Actual Test 10

TOEIC® Speaking

Speaking Test Directions

This is the TOEIC Speaking Test. This test includes eleven questions that measure different aspects of your speaking ability. The test lasts approximately 20 minutes.

Question	Task	Evaluation Criteria
1-2	Read a text aloud	• pronunciation • intonation and stress
3	Describe a picture	all of the above, plus • grammar • vocabulary • cohesion
4-6	Respond to questions	all of the above, plus • relevance of content • completeness of content
7-9	Respond to questions using information provided	all of the above
10	Propose a solution	all of the above
11	Express an opinion	all of the above

For each type of question, you will be given specific directions, including the time allowed for preparation and speaking.

It is to your advantage to say as much as you can in the time allowed. It is also important that you speak clearly and that you answer each question according to the directions.

Click on **Continue** to go on.

TOEIC® Speaking

Questions 1-2: Read a text aloud

Directions: In this part of the test, you will read aloud the text on the screen. You will have 45 seconds to prepare. Then you will have 45 seconds to read the text aloud.

TOEIC® Speaking

Question 1 of 11

We need an assistant manager in the promotion campaign for Shining Hair Shampoo. A bachelor's degree in business administration or marketing is necessary including at least three years of experience in a related field. We will offer high wages, generous welfare packages and 30 days off a year. Anyone who is interested in this position, please send your résumé by January 15th to shiningworkers@gmail.com. We are eager to find partners who are willing to dedicate themselves to growing with us.

PREPARATION TIME
00:00:45

RESPONSE TIME
00:00:45

TOEIC® Speaking

Question 2 of 11

Multi Packs Magazine Service will give you full complimentary services with a magazine subscription. If you want to be our subscriber, please download the form on the website and fill it out. You will be awarded 10,000 mileage points. They will be saved to your own account once you sign up. Also you will receive one free book voucher as a present. Your subscription will be automatically renewed until you cancel your subscription. This offer is valid for this month only. Please hurry up.

PREPARATION TIME
00:00:45

RESPONSE TIME
00:00:45

TOEIC® Speaking

Question 3: Describe a picture

Directions: In this part of the test, you will describe the picture on your screen in as much detail as you can. You will have 30 seconds to prepare your response. Then you will have 45 seconds to speak about the picture.

TOEIC® Speaking

Question 3 of 11

PREPARATION TIME
00:00:30

RESPONSE TIME
00:00:45

TOEIC® Speaking

Questions 4-6: Respond to questions

Directions: In this part of the test, you will answer three questions. For each question, begin responding immediately after you hear a beep. No preparation time is provided. You will have 15 seconds to respond to Questions 4 and 5 and 30 seconds to respond to Question 6.

TOEIC® Speaking — **Question 4 of 11**

Imagine that a Canadian marketing firm is doing research in your country. You have agreed to participate in a telephone interview about books.

How many books do you read per month and what kinds of books do you like to read?

RESPONSE TIME
00:00:15

TOEIC® Speaking — **Question 5 of 11**

Imagine that a Canadian marketing firm is doing research in your country. You have agreed to participate in a telephone interview about books.

Where do you usually buy books?

RESPONSE TIME
00:00:15

TOEIC® Speaking — **Question 6 of 11**

Imagine that a Canadian marketing firm is doing research in your country. You have agreed to participate in a telephone interview about books.

Do you think that books are better materials to get information from than other tools?

RESPONSE TIME
00:00:30

Questions 7-9: Respond to questions using information provided

Directions: In this part of the test, you will answer three questions based on the information provided. You will have 30 seconds to read the information before the questions begin. For each question, begin responding immediately after you hear a beep. No additional preparation time is provided. You will have 15 seconds to respond to Questions 7 and 8 and 30 seconds to respond to Question 9.

Pitt Brown

pittbrown@gmail.com

Objective: To obtain a position as a Marketing Director at Present Company

Experience

2008. 9 ~ Present	Next Mobile Co., USA, Media Assistant Manager
2004. 2 ~ 2006. 8	Number 1, Korea, Market Researcher
2000. 9 ~ 2004. 1	Crooger Computer, Inc., Korea, Advertising and Marketing Assistant

Education

2000. 12	Graduate of Southwest Missouri State University
	B.A. Marketing, emphasis Advertising and Promotion
	B.A. Mass Media, Journalism and Mass Communication

Abilities

Language	Fluent in Korean, English and French
Character	Excellent interpersonal skills, have an open mind, leadership abilities

PREPARATION TIME
00:00:30

Question 7 of 11

Pitt Brown
pittbrown@gmail.com

Objective: To obtain a position as a Marketing Director at Present Company

Experience

2008. 9 ~ Present	Next Mobile Co., USA, Media Assistant Manager
2004. 2 ~ 2006. 8	Number 1, Korea, Market Researcher
2000. 9 ~ 2004. 1	Crooger Computer, Inc., Korea, Advertising and Marketing Assistant

Education

2000. 12	Graduate of Southwest Missouri State University
	B.A. Marketing, emphasis Advertising and Promotion
	B.A. Mass Media, Journalism and Mass Communication

Abilities

Language	Fluent in Korean, English and French
Character	Excellent interpersonal skills, have an open mind, leadership abilities

RESPONSE TIME 00:00:15

Question 8 of 11

Pitt Brown
pittbrown@gmail.com

Objective: To obtain a position as a Marketing Director at Present Company

Experience

2008. 9 ~ Present	Next Mobile Co., USA, Media Assistant Manager
2004. 2 ~ 2006. 8	Number 1, Korea, Market Researcher
2000. 9 ~ 2004. 1	Crooger Computer, Inc., Korea, Advertising and Marketing Assistant

Education

2000. 12	Graduate of Southwest Missouri State University
	B.A. Marketing, emphasis Advertising and Promotion
	B.A. Mass Media, Journalism and Mass Communication

Abilities

Language	Fluent in Korean, English and French
Character	Excellent interpersonal skills, have an open mind, leadership abilities

RESPONSE TIME 00:00:15

Question 10: Propose a solution

Directions: In this part of the test, you will be presented with a problem and asked to propose a solution. You will have 30 seconds to prepare. Then you will have 60 seconds to speak.

In your response, be sure to
- show that you recognize the problem, and
- propose a way of dealing with the problem.

Question 9 of 11

Pitt Brown

pittbrown@gmail.com

Objective: To obtain a position as a Marketing Director at Present Company

Experience

2008. 9 ~ Present	Next Mobile Co., USA, Media Assistant Manager
2004. 2 ~ 2006. 8	Number 1, Korea, Market Researcher
2000. 9 ~ 2004. 1	Crooger Computer, Inc., Korea, Advertising and Marketing Assistant

Education

2000. 12	Graduate of Southwest Missouri State University
	B.A. Marketing, emphasis Advertising and Promotion
	B.A. Mass Media, Journalism and Mass Communication

Abilities

Language	Fluent in Korean, English and French
Character	Excellent interpersonal skills, have an open mind, leadership abilities

RESPONSE TIME
00:00:30

TOEIC® Speaking

Question 10 of 11

TOEIC® Speaking

Question 10 of 11

In your response, be sure to
- show that you recognize the problem, and
- propose a way of dealing with the problem.

PREPARATION TIME
00:00:30

RESPONSE TIME
00:01:00

TOEIC® Speaking

Question 11: Express an opinion

Directions: In this part of the test, you will give your opinion about a specific topic. Be sure to say as much as you can in the time allowed. You will have 15 seconds to prepare. Then you will have 60 seconds to speak.

TOEIC® Speaking

Question 11 of 11

What do you think is the most important skill which parents should teach their children? Please support your opinion with some reasons or examples.

- Communication skills
- How to spend money
- Independence

PREPARATION TIME
00:00:15

RESPONSE TIME
00:01:00

Actual Test 11

TOEIC® Speaking

Speaking Test Directions

This is the TOEIC Speaking Test. This test includes eleven questions that measure different aspects of your speaking ability. The test lasts approximately 20 minutes.

Question	Task	Evaluation Criteria
1-2	Read a text aloud	• pronunciation • intonation and stress
3	Describe a picture	all of the above, plus • grammar • vocabulary • cohesion
4-6	Respond to questions	all of the above, plus • relevance of content • completeness of content
7-9	Respond to questions using information provided	all of the above
10	Propose a solution	all of the above
11	Express an opinion	all of the above

For each type of question, you will be given specific directions, including the time allowed for preparation and speaking.

It is to your advantage to say as much as you can in the time allowed. It is also important that you speak clearly and that you answer each question according to the directions.

Click on **Continue** to go on.

TOEIC® Speaking

Questions 1-2: Read a text aloud

Directions: In this part of the test, you will read aloud the text on the screen. You will have 45 seconds to prepare. Then you will have 45 seconds to read the text aloud.

TOEIC® Speaking

Question 1 of 11

Vital Supplement Company is informing revised service charging principles to our sales staff. Our rates will increase slightly due to the raise in the wages of deliverymen. Presently we charge $3 for inbound shipping and $6 for outbound shipping. But this will increase to $4 and $8 each. Please don't forget to let all your own customers know before they order our products.

PREPARATION TIME
00:00:45

RESPONSE TIME
00:00:45

TOEIC® Speaking

Question 2 of 11

Hello, you have reached the office of Tom; I will be out of my office starting on Tuesday, October 18th. And I will be returning on Monday, October 24th. You can call me when I return or leave your name and number, then I will call you as soon as I return. If this is an emergency, I can be reached on my cell at 212-544-2578.

PREPARATION TIME
00:00:45

RESPONSE TIME
00:00:45

TOEIC® Speaking

Question 3: Describe a picture

Directions: In this part of the test, you will describe the picture on your screen in as much detail as you can. You will have 30 seconds to prepare your response. Then you will have 45 seconds to speak about the picture.

TOEIC® Speaking

Question 3 of 11

PREPARATION TIME
00:00:30

RESPONSE TIME
00:00:45

TOEIC® Speaking

Questions 4-6: Respond to questions

Directions: In this part of the test, you will answer three questions. For each question, begin responding immediately after you hear a beep. No preparation time is provided. You will have 15 seconds to respond to Questions 4 and 5 and 30 seconds to respond to Question 6.

TOEIC® Speaking — **Question 4 of 11**

Imagine that an Australian marketing firm is doing research in your country. You have agreed to participate in a telephone interview about perfume.

How often do you put on perfume?

RESPONSE TIME
00:00:15

TOEIC® Speaking — **Question 5 of 11**

Imagine that an Australian marketing firm is doing research in your country. You have agreed to participate in a telephone interview about perfume.

Do you think perfume is a good present for someone?

RESPONSE TIME
00:00:15

TOEIC® Speaking — **Question 6 of 11**

Imagine that an Australian marketing firm is doing research in your country. You have agreed to participate in a telephone interview about perfume.

What do you consider when you buy perfume?

RESPONSE TIME
00:00:30

Questions 7-9: Respond to questions using information provided

Directions: In this part of the test, you will answer three questions based on the information provided. You will have 30 seconds to read the information before the questions begin. For each question, begin responding immediately after you hear a beep. No additional preparation time is provided. You will have 15 seconds to respond to Questions 7 and 8 and 30 seconds to respond to Question 9.

Melbourne University Annual Literary Society

September 20th, 2013
Phillip Conference Hall, Starwood Hotel

Time	Activity	Speaker
9:00~9:30	Welcome Speech	George Corner
9:40~10:40	Guest Speaking: Copyright on the Internet	Rose Purple
10:50~11:50	Presentation: The Needs of Readers	Kelly Light
12:00~1:00	Lunch	
1:00~2:20	Writing Training: How to Write a Poem	Christine Port
2:30~3:50	Presentation: The Best Essay of 2013	Elaine Lee
4:00~5:00	Video Lecture: New Stream of Novel Writing	Tony Robinson

PREPARATION TIME
00:00:30

Melbourne University Annual Literary Society

September 20th, 2013
Phillip Conference Hall, Starwood Hotel

Time	Activity	Speaker
9:00~9:30	Welcome Speech	George Corner
9:40~10:40	Guest Speaking: Copyright on the Internet	Rose Purple
10:50~11:50	Presentation: The Needs of Readers	Kelly Light
12:00~1:00	Lunch	
1:00~2:20	Writing Training: How to Write a Poem	Christine Port
2:30~3:50	Presentation: The Best Essay of 2013	Elaine Lee
4:00~5:00	Video Lecture: New Stream of Novel Writing	Tony Robinson

RESPONSE TIME
00:00:15

Melbourne University Annual Literary Society

September 20th, 2013
Phillip Conference Hall, Starwood Hotel

Time	Activity	Speaker
9:00~9:30	Welcome Speech	George Corner
9:40~10:40	Guest Speaking: Copyright on the Internet	Rose Purple
10:50~11:50	Presentation: The Needs of Readers	Kelly Light
12:00~1:00	Lunch	
1:00~2:20	Writing Training: How to Write a Poem	Christine Port
2:30~3:50	Presentation: The Best Essay of 2013	Elaine Lee
4:00~5:00	Video Lecture: New Stream of Novel Writing	Tony Robinson

RESPONSE TIME
00:00:15

Question 10: Propose a solution

Directions: In this part of the test, you will be presented with a problem and asked to propose a solution. You will have 30 seconds to prepare. Then you will have 60 seconds to speak.

In your response, be sure to
- show that you recognize the problem, and
- propose a way of dealing with the problem.

Melbourne University Annual Literary Society

September 20th, 2013
Phillip Conference Hall, Starwood Hotel

Time	Activity	Speaker
9:00~9:30	Welcome Speech	George Corner
9:40~10:40	Guest Speaking: Copyright on the Internet	Rose Purple
10:50~11:50	Presentation: The Needs of Readers	Kelly Light
12:00~1:00	Lunch	
1:00~2:20	Writing Training: How to Write a Poem	Christine Port
2:30~3:50	Presentation: The Best Essay of 2013	Elaine Lee
4:00~5:00	Video Lecture: New Stream of Novel Writing	Tony Robinson

RESPONSE TIME
00:00:30

TOEIC® Speaking

Question 11: Express an opinion

Directions: In this part of the test, you will give your opinion about a specific topic. Be sure to say as much as you can in the time allowed. You will have 15 seconds to prepare. Then you will have 60 seconds to speak.

TOEIC® Speaking

Question 11 of 11

Do you agree or disagree with this statement?

These days more and more people use electronic books than printed books. And some people say that printed books will disappear in the near future.

Please support your opinion with some reasons or examples.

PREPARATION TIME
00:00:15

RESPONSE TIME
00:01:00

TOEIC® Speaking

Question 10 of 11

TOEIC® Speaking

Question 10 of 11

In your response, be sure to

- show that you recognize the problem, and
- propose a way of dealing with the problem.

PREPARATION TIME
00:00:30

RESPONSE TIME
00:01:00

Actual Test 12

TOEIC® Speaking

Speaking Test Directions

This is the TOEIC Speaking Test. This test includes eleven questions that measure different aspects of your speaking ability. The test lasts approximately 20 minutes.

Question	Task	Evaluation Criteria
1-2	Read a text aloud	• pronunciation • intonation and stress
3	Describe a picture	all of the above, plus • grammar • vocabulary • cohesion
4-6	Respond to questions	all of the above, plus • relevance of content • completeness of content
7-9	Respond to questions using information provided	all of the above
10	Propose a solution	all of the above
11	Express an opinion	all of the above

For each type of question, you will be given specific directions, including the time allowed for preparation and speaking.

It is to your advantage to say as much as you can in the time allowed. It is also important that you speak clearly and that you answer each question according to the directions.

Click on **Continue** to go on.

TOEIC® Speaking

Questions 1-2: Read a text aloud

Directions: In this part of the test, you will read aloud the text on the screen. You will have 45 seconds to prepare. Then you will have 45 seconds to read the text aloud.

TOEIC® Speaking

Question 1 of 11

US Airline has recently invested more than $500 million to enhance our customers' flying experience. We plan to roll out more flat-bed seats in our US Global and Travel First cabins. In addition, we will be adding Wi-Fi to more than 200 Boeing 717 and 747 aircraft as well as expanding Economy Plus across the entire mainline fleet.

PREPARATION TIME
00:00:45

RESPONSE TIME
00:00:45

TOEIC® Speaking

Question 2 of 11

Make your job search easier. Get the job recommendations from Career Builder! Our patent-pending job matching technology targets jobs that match keywords in your résumé, the jobs you view and ultimately the jobs you apply for. The more you use Careerbuilder.com, the better the job matches become.

PREPARATION TIME
00:00:45

RESPONSE TIME
00:00:45

TOEIC® Speaking

Question 3: Describe a picture

Directions: In this part of the test, you will describe the picture on your screen in as much detail as you can. You will have 30 seconds to prepare your response. Then you will have 45 seconds to speak about the picture.

TOEIC® Speaking

Question 3 of 11

PREPARATION TIME
00:00:30

RESPONSE TIME
00:00:45

TOEIC® Speaking

Questions 4-6: Respond to questions

Directions: In this part of the test, you will answer three questions. For each question, begin responding immediately after you hear a beep. No preparation time is provided. You will have 15 seconds to respond to Questions 4 and 5 and 30 seconds to respond to Question 6.

TOEIC® Speaking — **Question 4 of 11**

Imagine that an American marketing firm is doing research in your country. You have agreed to participate in a telephone interview about meetings.

When was the last time you attended a meeting?

RESPONSE TIME
00:00:15

TOEIC® Speaking — **Question 5 of 11**

Imagine that an American marketing firm is doing research in your country. You have agreed to participate in a telephone interview about meetings.

What do you commonly do beforehand to prepare for a meeting?

RESPONSE TIME
00:00:15

TOEIC® Speaking — **Question 6 of 11**

Imagine that an American marketing firm is doing research in your country. You have agreed to participate in a telephone interview about meetings.

Do you think people should wear formal suits to attend a meeting?

RESPONSE TIME
00:00:30

TOEIC® Speaking

Questions 7-9: Respond to questions using information provided

Directions: In this part of the test, you will answer three questions based on the information provided. You will have 30 seconds to read the information before the questions begin. For each question, begin responding immediately after you hear a beep. No additional preparation time is provided. You will have 15 seconds to respond to Questions 7 and 8 and 30 seconds to respond to Question 9.

TOEIC® Speaking

How to Start a Business

Rich Carton Hotel
25th August 2013

8:00 a.m.	Registration of Participants
8:45 a.m.	Welcome & Opening Ceremony
9:00 a.m.	Keynote Speech on "A Supervisor's Success Story" by Michael Segal
10:00 a.m.	Break / Exhibition Fairs
10:30 a.m.	Plenary Session on "How to Overcome Several Cases of Failure"
12:00 p.m.	Lunch
12:30 p.m.	Presentation on "Research Update" by Billy Meier, Professor at Illinois State University
1:30 p.m.	Presentation on "How to Do Budget Planning for Business" by Lucy Owell, Professor at Horvard University
2:45 p.m.	Break / Exhibition Fairs
3:00 p.m.	Questions & Answers

PREPARATION TIME
00:00:30

How to Start a Business

Rich Carton Hotel
25th August 2013

Time	Event
8:00 a.m.	Registration of Participants
8:45 a.m.	Welcome & Opening Ceremony
9:00 a.m.	Keynote Speech on "A Supervisor's Success Story" by Michael Segal
10:00 a.m.	Break / Exhibition Fairs
10:30 a.m.	Plenary Session on "How to Overcome Several Cases of Failure"
12:00 p.m.	Lunch
12:30 p.m.	Presentation on "Research Update" by Billy Meier, Professor at Illinois State University
1:30 p.m.	Presentation on "How to Do Budget Planning for Business" by Lucy Owell, Professor at Horvard University
2:45 p.m.	Break / Exhibition Fairs
3:00 p.m.	Questions & Answers

RESPONSE TIME 00:00:15

How to Start a Business

Rich Carton Hotel
25th August 2013

Time	Event
8:00 a.m.	Registration of Participants
8:45 a.m.	Welcome & Opening Ceremony
9:00 a.m.	Keynote Speech on "A Supervisor's Success Story" by Michael Segal
10:00 a.m.	Break / Exhibition Fairs
10:30 a.m.	Plenary Session on "How to Overcome Several Cases of Failure"
12:00 p.m.	Lunch
12:30 p.m.	Presentation on "Research Update" by Billy Meier, Professor at Illinois State University
1:30 p.m.	Presentation on "How to Do Budget Planning for Business" by Lucy Owell, Professor at Horvard University
2:45 p.m.	Break / Exhibition Fairs
3:00 p.m.	Questions & Answers

RESPONSE TIME 00:00:15

Question 10: Propose a solution

Directions: In this part of the test, you will be presented with a problem and asked to propose a solution. You will have 30 seconds to prepare. Then you will have 60 seconds to speak.

In your response, be sure to
- show that you recognize the problem, and
- propose a way of dealing with the problem.

How to Start a Business

Rich Carton Hotel
25th August 2013

Time	Event
8:00 a.m.	Registration of Participants
8:45 a.m.	Welcome & Opening Ceremony
9:00 a.m.	Keynote Speech on "A Supervisor's Success Story" by Michael Segal
10:00 a.m.	Break / Exhibition Fairs
10:30 a.m.	Plenary Session on "How to Overcome Several Cases of Failure"
12:00 p.m.	Lunch
12:30 p.m.	Presentation on "Research Update" by Billy Meier, Professor at Illinois State University
1:30 p.m.	Presentation on "How to Do Budget Planning for Business" by Lucy Owell, Professor at Horvard University
2:45 p.m.	Break / Exhibition Fairs
3:00 p.m.	Questions & Answers

RESPONSE TIME
00:00:30

Question 11: Express an opinion

Directions: In this part of the test, you will give your opinion about a specific topic. Be sure to say as much as you can in the time allowed. You will have 15 seconds to prepare. Then you will have 60 seconds to speak.

Question 11 of 11

What do you think is the most important factor for success in business? Choose one and support your opinion with reasons or examples.

- Customer service
- Technology
- Capital

PREPARATION TIME
00:00:15

RESPONSE TIME
00:01:00

Question 10 of 11

Question 10 of 11

In your response, be sure to
- show that you recognize the problem, and
- propose a way of dealing with the problem.

PREPARATION TIME
00:00:30

RESPONSE TIME
00:01:00

Actual Test 13

Speaking Test Directions

This is the TOEIC Speaking Test. This test includes eleven questions that measure different aspects of your speaking ability. The test lasts approximately 20 minutes.

Question	Task	Evaluation Criteria
1-2	Read a text aloud	• pronunciation • intonation and stress
3	Describe a picture	all of the above, plus • grammar • vocabulary • cohesion
4-6	Respond to questions	all of the above, plus • relevance of content • completeness of content
7-9	Respond to questions using information provided	all of the above
10	Propose a solution	all of the above
11	Express an opinion	all of the above

For each type of question, you will be given specific directions, including the time allowed for preparation and speaking.

It is to your advantage to say as much as you can in the time allowed. It is also important that you speak clearly and that you answer each question according to the directions.

Click on **Continue** to go on.

Questions 1-2: Read a text aloud

Directions: In this part of the test, you will read aloud the text on the screen. You will have 45 seconds to prepare. Then you will have 45 seconds to read the text aloud.

TOEIC® Speaking — Question 1 of 11

Priceline is the only place where you can shop and compare from over 165,000 hotels around the world. You can select your exact hotel and price. View thousands of hotel reviews submitted by customers just like you who want to get a top quality hotel stay at a discount price. You can be sure you're getting the lowest rate at top-notch hotels.

PREPARATION TIME
00:00:45

RESPONSE TIME
00:00:45

TOEIC® Speaking — Question 2 of 11

Global Vision is looking for the qualified candidates to fill in the following positions: agriculture trainer in Bangkok, finance officer in Hong Kong, and livestock trainer in Shanghai. For details, please visit www.brightglob.com. The deadline for applications is July 21, 2013. Only the short-listed candidates will be contacted.

PREPARATION TIME
00:00:45

RESPONSE TIME
00:00:45

TOEIC® Speaking

Question 3: Describe a picture

Directions: In this part of the test, you will describe the picture on your screen in as much detail as you can. You will have 30 seconds to prepare your response. Then you will have 45 seconds to speak about the picture.

TOEIC® Speaking — Question 3 of 11

PREPARATION TIME
00:00:30

RESPONSE TIME
00:00:45

TOEIC® Speaking

Questions 4-6: Respond to questions

Directions: In this part of the test, you will answer three questions. For each question, begin responding immediately after you hear a beep. No preparation time is provided. You will have 15 seconds to respond to Questions 4 and 5 and 30 seconds to respond to Question 6.

TOEIC® Speaking — **Question 4 of 11**

Imagine that a British marketing firm is doing research in your country. You have agreed to participate in a telephone interview about getting a job.

What is your occupation or what type of job are you looking for?

RESPONSE TIME
00:00:15

TOEIC® Speaking — **Question 5 of 11**

Imagine that a British marketing firm is doing research in your country. You have agreed to participate in a telephone interview about getting a job.

Where do you get information on a job opening?

RESPONSE TIME
00:00:15

TOEIC® Speaking — **Question 6 of 11**

Imagine that a British marketing firm is doing research in your country. You have agreed to participate in a telephone interview about getting a job.

What do you think a school should teach to students for their future jobs?

- Scientific knowledge
- Multi-tasking skills
- Driving force

RESPONSE TIME
00:00:30

TOEIC® Speaking

Questions 7-9: Respond to questions using information provided

Directions: In this part of the test, you will answer three questions based on the information provided. You will have 30 seconds to read the information before the questions begin. For each question, begin responding immediately after you hear a beep. No additional preparation time is provided. You will have 15 seconds to respond to Questions 7 and 8 and 30 seconds to respond to Question 9.

TOEIC® Speaking

ELIZABETH QUEENS HOTEL

Room Types	Description	Room Rate*
Standard Twin	two single beds	108 USD
Double-Double	two double beds, desk, sofa	120 USD
Executive Suite	one king-size bed, living room, balcony, Jacuzzi	289 USD

Services

Internet services $3/hour or $20 for one day
Room services   various, depending on guest's order
Laundry services   T-shirts, shirts $8; trousers, skirts $12

* A 15% discount is available to Elizabeth Queens Travel club members.
* A membership pass must be shown at the front desk when checking in.

PREPARATION TIME

00:00:30

ELIZABETH QUEENS HOTEL

Room Types	Description	Room Rate*
Standard Twin	two single beds	108 USD
Double-Double	two double beds, desk, sofa	120 USD
Executive Suite	one king-size bed, living room, balcony, Jacuzzi	289 USD

Services

Internet services	$3/hour or $20 for one day
Room services	various, depending on guest's order
Laundry services	T-shirts, shirts $8; trousers, skirts $12

* A 15% discount is available to Elizabeth Queens Travel club members.
* A membership pass must be shown at the front desk when checking in.

RESPONSE TIME
00:00:15

ELIZABETH QUEENS HOTEL

Room Types	Description	Room Rate*
Standard Twin	two single beds	108 USD
Double-Double	two double beds, desk, sofa	120 USD
Executive Suite	one king-size bed, living room, balcony, Jacuzzi	289 USD

Services

Internet services	$3/hour or $20 for one day
Room services	various, depending on guest's order
Laundry services	T-shirts, shirts $8; trousers, skirts $12

* A 15% discount is available to Elizabeth Queens Travel club members.
* A membership pass must be shown at the front desk when checking in.

RESPONSE TIME
00:00:15

Question 9 of 11

ELIZABETH QUEENS HOTEL

Room Types	Description	Room Rate*
Standard Twin	two single beds	108 USD
Double-Double	two double beds, desk, sofa	120 USD
Executive Suite	one king-size bed, living room, balcony, Jacuzzi	289 USD

Services

Internet services $3/hour or $20 for one day
Room services   various, depending on guest's order
Laundry services   T-shirts, shirts $8; trousers, skirts $12

* A 15% discount is available to Elizabeth Queens Travel club members.
* A membership pass must be shown at the front desk when checking in.

RESPONSE TIME
00:00:30

Question 10: Propose a solution

Directions: In this part of the test, you will be presented with a problem and asked to propose a solution. You will have 30 seconds to prepare. Then you will have 60 seconds to speak.

In your response, be sure to

- show that you recognize the problem, and
- propose a way of dealing with the problem.

TOEIC® Speaking

Question 11: Express an opinion

Directions: In this part of the test, you will give your opinion about a specific topic. Be sure to say as much as you can in the time allowed. You will have 15 seconds to prepare. Then you will have 60 seconds to speak.

TOEIC® Speaking

Question 11 of 11

Which do you like better, working as a salesperson or office worker? Please support your opinion with reasons or examples.

PREPARATION TIME
00:00:15

RESPONSE TIME
00:01:00

TOEIC® Speaking

Question 10 of 11

TOEIC® Speaking

Question 10 of 11

In your response, be sure to
- show that you recognize the problem, and
- propose a way of dealing with the problem.

PREPARATION TIME
00:00:30

RESPONSE TIME
00:01:00

Actual Test 14

TOEIC® Speaking

Speaking Test Directions

This is the TOEIC Speaking Test. This test includes eleven questions that measure different aspects of your speaking ability. The test lasts approximately 20 minutes.

Question	Task	Evaluation Criteria
1-2	Read a text aloud	• pronunciation • intonation and stress
3	Describe a picture	all of the above, plus • grammar • vocabulary • cohesion
4-6	Respond to questions	all of the above, plus • relevance of content • completeness of content
7-9	Respond to questions using information provided	all of the above
10	Propose a solution	all of the above
11	Express an opinion	all of the above

For each type of question, you will be given specific directions, including the time allowed for preparation and speaking.

It is to your advantage to say as much as you can in the time allowed. It is also important that you speak clearly and that you answer each question according to the directions.

Click on **Continue** to go on.

TOEIC® Speaking

Questions 1-2: Read a text aloud

Directions: In this part of the test, you will read aloud the text on the screen. You will have 45 seconds to prepare. Then you will have 45 seconds to read the text aloud.

TOEIC® Speaking

Question 1 of 11

Sitter canceled last night? No problem. With our Care-on-Call feature, it's easy to find trustworthy caregivers and contact them in seconds. Mostcare.com not only gives you the flexibility to find a caregiver whose schedule fits yours, but also the convenience of having your sitter come to you.

PREPARATION TIME 00:00:45

RESPONSE TIME 00:00:45

TOEIC® Speaking

Question 2 of 11

When you embark on a European voyage with Ajar Club Cruises, romance is never far away. It's easy to explore the history and culture of the most beautiful destinations in the world. Take a relaxing trip on a canal boat in Amsterdam, soak up some sun on the beautiful beaches, get a closer look at legendary Renaissance art in Italy.

PREPARATION TIME 00:00:45

RESPONSE TIME 00:00:45

TOEIC® Speaking

Question 3: Describe a picture

Directions: In this part of the test, you will describe the picture on your screen in as much detail as you can. You will have 30 seconds to prepare your response. Then you will have 45 seconds to speak about the picture.

TOEIC® Speaking

Question 3 of 11

PREPARATION TIME 00:00:30

RESPONSE TIME 00:00:45

TOEIC® Speaking

Questions 4-6: Respond to questions

Directions: In this part of the test, you will answer three questions. For each question, begin responding immediately after you hear a beep. No preparation time is provided. You will have 15 seconds to respond to Questions 4 and 5 and 30 seconds to respond to Question 6.

TOEIC® Speaking — **Question 4 of 11**

Imagine that an Australian marketing firm is doing research in your country. You have agreed to participate in a telephone interview about vacations.

Where do you usually go for your vacation?

RESPONSE TIME
00:00:15

TOEIC® Speaking — **Question 5 of 11**

Imagine that an Australian marketing firm is doing research in your country. You have agreed to participate in a telephone interview about vacations.

How many bags do you carry when you take a trip?

RESPONSE TIME
00:00:15

TOEIC® Speaking — **Question 6 of 11**

Imagine that an Australian marketing firm is doing research in your country. You have agreed to participate in a telephone interview about vacations.

Are you willing to pay for getting guidance from a travel guide?

RESPONSE TIME
00:00:30

TOEIC® Speaking

Questions 7-9: Respond to questions using information provided

Directions: In this part of the test, you will answer three questions based on the information provided. You will have 30 seconds to read the information before the questions begin. For each question, begin responding immediately after you hear a beep. No additional preparation time is provided. You will have 15 seconds to respond to Questions 7 and 8 and 30 seconds to respond to Question 9.

TOEIC® Speaking

Fast Copy Printing Company

· Order Date: Sep. 12th
· Pick up Date: Sep. 20th

Item	Type	Print	Amount	Price ($)
Brochures	White paper	Both sides	200	10
Posters	Glossy paper	One side	500	30
Posters	Color paper (blue)	One side	300	20
			1,000	60
			10% Discount	-6
			TOTAL	54

● All customers who order 700 or more brochures or posters totally can receive a 10% discount off the total price.

PREPARATION TIME
00:00:30

Fast Copy Printing Company

- Order Date: Sep. 12th
- Pick up Date: Sep. 20th

Item	Type	Print	Amount	Price ($)
Brochures	White paper	Both sides	200	10
Posters	Glossy paper	One side	500	30
Posters	Color paper (blue)	One side	300	20
			1,000	60
			10% Discount	-6
			TOTAL	54

- All customers who order 700 or more brochures or posters totally can receive a 10% discount off the total price.

RESPONSE TIME
00:00:15

Fast Copy Printing Company

- Order Date: Sep. 12th
- Pick up Date: Sep. 20th

Item	Type	Print	Amount	Price ($)
Brochures	White paper	Both sides	200	10
Posters	Glossy paper	One side	500	30
Posters	Color paper (blue)	One side	300	20
			1,000	60
			10% Discount	-6
			TOTAL	54

- All customers who order 700 or more brochures or posters totally can receive a 10% discount off the total price.

RESPONSE TIME
00:00:15

Question 10: Propose a solution

Directions: In this part of the test, you will be presented with a problem and asked to propose a solution. You will have 30 seconds to prepare. Then you will have 60 seconds to speak.

In your response, be sure to
- show that you recognize the problem, and
- propose a way of dealing with the problem.

Fast Copy Printing Company

- Order Date: Sep. 12th
- Pick up Date: Sep. 20th

Item	Type	Print	Amount	Price ($)
Brochures	White paper	Both sides	200	10
Posters	Glossy paper	One side	500	30
Posters	Color paper (blue)	One side	300	20
			1,000	60
			10% Discount	-6
			TOTAL	54

● All customers who order 700 or more brochures or posters totally can receive a 10% discount off the total price.

RESPONSE TIME
00:00:30

Question 11: Express an opinion

Directions: In this part of the test, you will give your opinion about a specific topic. Be sure to say as much as you can in the time allowed. You will have 15 seconds to prepare. Then you will have 60 seconds to speak.

Question 11 of 11

Do you think children nowadays have more interest in international issues than children in the past? Why? Please support your opinion with some reasons or examples.

PREPARATION TIME
00:00:15

RESPONSE TIME
00:01:00

Question 10 of 11

Question 10 of 11

In your response, be sure to
- show that you recognize the problem, and
- propose a way of dealing with the problem.

PREPARATION TIME
00:00:30

RESPONSE TIME
00:01:00

Actual Test 15

TOEIC® Speaking

Speaking Test Directions

This is the TOEIC Speaking Test. This test includes eleven questions that measure different aspects of your speaking ability. The test lasts approximately 20 minutes.

Question	Task	Evaluation Criteria
1-2	Read a text aloud	• pronunciation • intonation and stress
3	Describe a picture	all of the above, plus • grammar • vocabulary • cohesion
4-6	Respond to questions	all of the above, plus • relevance of content • completeness of content
7-9	Respond to questions using information provided	all of the above
10	Propose a solution	all of the above
11	Express an opinion	all of the above

For each type of question, you will be given specific directions, including the time allowed for preparation and speaking.

It is to your advantage to say as much as you can in the time allowed. It is also important that you speak clearly and that you answer each question according to the directions.

Click on **Continue** to go on.

TOEIC® Speaking

Questions 1-2: Read a text aloud

Directions: In this part of the test, you will read aloud the text on the screen. You will have 45 seconds to prepare. Then you will have 45 seconds to read the text aloud.

TOEIC® Speaking

Question 1 of 11

Not a member yet? Join Mileage Plus. Begin earning award miles for things you do every day. Members earn award miles by flying United or Star Alliance airlines and by purchasing products or services from a wide variety of partners worldwide. Members use award miles for travel, hotel and car rental, plus everyday purchases and activities.

PREPARATION TIME
00:00:45

RESPONSE TIME
00:00:45

TOEIC® Speaking

Question 2 of 11

This is the download site for sample résumés. All the résumés are free to use as models for your own. Please select the file you wish to download and the service you wish to use. If you have any problems accessing the files or any of the service links are dead, please let us know at the bottom of the page.

PREPARATION TIME
00:00:45

RESPONSE TIME
00:00:45

TOEIC® Speaking

Question 3: Describe a picture

Directions: In this part of the test, you will describe the picture on your screen in as much detail as you can. You will have 30 seconds to prepare your response. Then you will have 45 seconds to speak about the picture.

TOEIC® Speaking

Question 3 of 11

PREPARATION TIME
00:00:30

RESPONSE TIME
00:00:45

TOEIC® Speaking

Questions 4-6: Respond to questions

Directions: In this part of the test, you will answer three questions. For each question, begin responding immediately after you hear a beep. No preparation time is provided. You will have 15 seconds to respond to Questions 4 and 5 and 30 seconds to respond to Question 6.

TOEIC® Speaking — **Question 4 of 11**

Imagine that a Canadian marketing firm is doing research in your country. You have agreed to participate in a telephone interview about high school.

What kinds of books did you like to read in your high school days?

RESPONSE TIME
00:00:15

TOEIC® Speaking — **Question 5 of 11**

Imagine that a Canadian marketing firm is doing research in your country. You have agreed to participate in a telephone interview about high school.

What kinds of sports made your high school famous?

RESPONSE TIME
00:00:15

TOEIC® Speaking — **Question 6 of 11**

Imagine that a Canadian marketing firm is doing research in your country. You have agreed to participate in a telephone interview about high school.

Which do you prefer between a small high school and a big high school?

RESPONSE TIME
00:00:30

TOEIC® Speaking

Questions 7-9: Respond to questions using information provided

Directions: In this part of the test, you will answer three questions based on the information provided. You will have 30 seconds to read the information before the questions begin. For each question, begin responding immediately after you hear a beep. No additional preparation time is provided. You will have 15 seconds to respond to Questions 7 and 8 and 30 seconds to respond to Question 9.

TOEIC® Speaking

Thunderstorm Delivered Groceries Inc.

301-372-3663

Check our schedule to find your weekly order day and delivery day.

Delivery Area	Order Day	Delivery Day
Prince George's County	Monday	Wednesday
Charles County	Monday	Wednesday
Washington D.C.	Tuesday	Thursday
Montgomery County	Wednesday	Friday

- Call between 9 a.m. and 4 p.m. on your designated call-in day.
- Minimum order: $25.00 (excluding service charge)

PREPARATION TIME

00:00:30

111

Question 7 of 11

Thunderstorm Delivered Groceries Inc.

301-372-3663

Check our schedule to find your weekly order day and delivery day.

Delivery Area	Order Day	Delivery Day
Prince George's County	Monday	Wednesday
Charles County	Monday	Wednesday
Washington D.C.	Tuesday	Thursday
Montgomery County	Wednesday	Friday

- Call between 9 a.m. and 4 p.m. on your designated call-in day.
- Minimum order: $25.00 (excluding service charge)

RESPONSE TIME
00:00:15

Question 8 of 11

Thunderstorm Delivered Groceries Inc.

301-372-3663

Check our schedule to find your weekly order day and delivery day.

Delivery Area	Order Day	Delivery Day
Prince George's County	Monday	Wednesday
Charles County	Monday	Wednesday
Washington D.C.	Tuesday	Thursday
Montgomery County	Wednesday	Friday

- Call between 9 a.m. and 4 p.m. on your designated call-in day.
- Minimum order: $25.00 (excluding service charge)

RESPONSE TIME
00:00:15

Question 10: Propose a solution

Directions: In this part of the test, you will be presented with a problem and asked to propose a solution. You will have 30 seconds to prepare. Then you will have 60 seconds to speak.

In your response, be sure to
- show that you recognize the problem, and
- propose a way of dealing with the problem.

Question 9 of 11

Thunderstorm Delivered Groceries Inc.

301-372-3663

Check our schedule to find your weekly order day and delivery day.

Delivery Area	Order Day	Delivery Day
Prince George's County	Monday	Wednesday
Charles County	Monday	Wednesday
Washington D.C.	Tuesday	Thursday
Montgomery County	Wednesday	Friday

- Call between 9 a.m. and 4 p.m. on your designated call-in day.
- Minimum order: $25.00 (excluding service charge)

RESPONSE TIME
00:00:30

Question 11: Express an opinion

Directions: In this part of the test, you will give your opinion about a specific topic. Be sure to say as much as you can in the time allowed. You will have 15 seconds to prepare. Then you will have 60 seconds to speak.

Question 11 of 11

Imagine you have to cut your personal budget next year. What kinds of expenditures can you save on first?

- Clothing shopping
- Cultural life
- Health and exercise

PREPARATION TIME 00:00:15

RESPONSE TIME 00:01:00

Question 10 of 11

Question 10 of 11

In your response, be sure to
- show that you recognize the problem, and
- propose a way of dealing with the problem.

PREPARATION TIME 00:00:30

RESPONSE TIME 00:01:00

나혼자 끝내는 新토익 PART 1~4

신토익 실전 12회

더욱 까다로워진 신토익 대비와 함께 덤으로 청취력 향상까지!

- 신토익 LC 실전
  국내 최다 문제 수록
- 문제 + 스크립트 + 정답
  + 번역 + 해설 + 어휘가
  한 권에 수록
- 수험생들이
  가장 어려워하는
  영국식 발음 완벽 대비
- 실전용·복습용·고사장
  버전 MP3 무료 다운로드
  QR 코드 & 홈페이지

신토익 실전 12회 수록 | 이주은 지음 | 2017년 3월 출간 | 424페이지 | MP3 무료다운로드

나혼자 끝내는 新토익 PART 5&6

신토익 실전 12회

토익 고득점을 위해 필히 정복해야 하는 PART 5&6

- 틀린 문제는 다시는 틀리지 않도록 훈련하는 체계적 구성
- 스스로 점검하고 보완할 수 있는 나혼토 체크 리스트 제공
- 저자 직강의 무료 음성 강의 지원
- 어휘 리스트 & 테스트 제공

신토익 실전 12회 수록 | 박혜원, 전보람 지음 | 2017년 2월 출간 | 257페이지

나혼자 끝내는 新토익 PART 7

신토익 실전 10회

저자 직강 PART 7 공략법 제공

신토익 고득점을 결정하는 PART 7 필수 정복 코스

PART 7 실전 10회 문제집 + 핵심 패러프레이징을 수록한 해설집 + 나혼토 1:1 저자 코칭

시간 관리가 더욱 중요해진 PART 7, 실전 훈련으로 완벽 대비!

- 더욱 까다로워진 신토익 PART 7 실전 10회분 수록
- 정답의 단서와 패러프레이징 원리를 수록한 해설집 수록
- 나혼토 1:1 저자 코칭
- 어휘 리스트 & 테스트 제공

신토익 실전 10회 수록 | 이미영, 박선영 지음 | 2017년 7월 출간 | 304 페이지

新 토익! 어떻게 시작해야 할지 몰라 망설이는 초보 수험생들을 위한

토익 초보·입문자 맞춤형 교재

나에게 꼭 맞는 토익 책은?

- ✓ 고등학교 졸업 이후 영어 공부를 해 본 적이 없다.
- ✓ 토익 시험이라곤 본 적이 없지만 신발 사이즈 점수가 나올 거 같다.
- ✓ 혼자서 공부하기 힘들어 동영상 강의가 필요하다.

↓
YES

초급자 맞춤형
동영상 강의 제공
총 24강

- ✓ 어느 정도 영어 공부는 해 왔지만 토익 공부는 해 본적이 없다.
- ✓ 모의토익 시험에서 500점 정도는 나온다.
- ✓ 당장 토익 시험을 앞두고 있으며 750점 이상 점수가 필요하다.

↓
YES

나혼자 끝내는 신토익 스타트 LC+RC | 넥서스토익연구소 지음 | 2018년 1월 출간 | 404페이지
나혼자 끝내는 신토익 BASIC LC+RC | 원정서, 넥서스토익연구소 지음 | 2017년 11월 출간 | 352 페이지